echoes *of* mercy

Testimony of a Prodigal's Mom

SUSAN HAMLIN

MEDIA.COM

Echoes of Mercy

Published by
Illumify Media Global
www.IllumifyMedia.com
"Let's bring your book to life!"

Paperback ISBN: 978-1-964251-50-9

Cover design by Debbie Lewis

Printed in the United States of America

Dedication

To Fig, my husband, lover, servant,
and gladsome editor.

To my daughter Miriam,
who lived with a squeaky wheel.
I'm loving the time with you.

To Nate. Because you want to warn others of Satan's
awful deception, you have exposed your life.
God bless you, son.

Contents

PART TWO
THOUGHTS FROM THE STORY

"Praise be to the God and Father of our Lord Jesus Christ, the Father of compassion and the God of all comfort, who comforts us in all our troubles, so that we can comfort those in any trouble with the comfort we ourselves have received from God."
(2 Corinthians 1:3–6)

Introduction

"Mamaw, tell me a story."
Visiting my daughter and her husband, I heard this urgent plea nightly from my three grandsons. Since my husband and I and our two children had lived in the western jungle of Papua New Guinea for many years, I had my choice of stomach-churning, hair-raising adventures.

What I tell you here trumps those bush tales. It's the true story of my boy Nate and how God has been a "merciful and gracious [Father] . . . abounding in steadfast love and faithfulness" (Exodus 34:6 ESV) to both this needy mother and her wandering son from the beginning to now. This account being from my perspective, I'll talk in terms of "my son," although my dear husband, Newton, who's "Fig" to me, is a large part of the story, and of getting it told.

Whether you, and your son or daughter, have suffered for months, a few years, or a great many years, the question is the same: Is God enough—sufficient to comfort us in our heartaches, able to rescue our children?

I am speaking primarily to mothers, as a believer in the God of the Bible. Through my experience, may you be encouraged to hang on to the God who cares tenderly for you, to trust in his steadfast love for that wayward child, and to believe his great and precious promises.

PART ONE

THE STORY

I

Tragedy

I was awakened early one morning in October 2002 by a call from our daughter, Miriam. Through tears she said that Nate, had been arrested for killing a man! I was in shock.

Lord, please, no, I begged.

Fig and I had taken him to supper just the night before, and there had been no talk of problems. What had happened? Who had been killed? What could have caused such a reaction in our son? I had nothing but questions, but Miriam had no answers.

I cried aloud, "Oh God, have mercy on Nate, and on the family who has lost a boy!"

A week later we saw Nate in jail and heard the story.

He and his girlfriend Heidi had gone to visit Kia, a friend of hers who lived nearby in a trailer park. Kia's little girl was playing in the yard when Nate, Heidi, and two of Nate's friends showed up. All but the little girl went inside. A while later the live-in boyfriend, Shawn, came home fussing about the child being outside alone. When Shawn walked in and passed Nate, he muttered something like, "I'm gonna kill you," referring to Kia, the mother, who was around the corner in the kitchen.

Nate had never met this guy, but he was ready to defend the woman if necessary. He heard a commotion in the kitchen, looked in and saw that the boyfriend had thrown Kia on the table and was beating her across her throat and face.

Nate went to her aid, but as Shawn turned on Nate, he drew a knife. As they wrestled, Nate took the knife from him, and stabbed him three times. He quickly grabbed his own girlfriend and ran out the door. The wounded man yelled after them, "I'm gonna get a gun and kill you." The victim did manage to get as far as the neighbor's house, but died there on the porch.

The stabbing could have ended Nate's life forever, but for the abundant mercy of God. This is the story of redemption, not from rags to riches, but from death to life, and from darkness to light. It's a story only God could have written in the lives of this son and his mom.

My testimony is of getting to know God, witnessing his faithfulness in the face of trouble.

Without Nate I would never have had the opportunity to prove that God is who he says he is.

Many of the things I had thought as a young mom, like *I could never live through that,* or *I could never do such and such,* I have lived through, and I have done. The difference is God, the living God, whose power is great, and whose steadfast love can be counted on.

2

The Beginning

Miriam, our first, born in 1974, was the dearest little girl. She didn't like getting into trouble, so was relatively easy to rear. When she was conceived, I thought it would naturally follow that we would have another baby. I was wrong. Waiting for a few months wasn't a big deal, but as time stretched on, I began to lose hope.

My longings frustrated, I asked God, *What are you doing?* He heard my cry, and as I prayed and read his Word, he began working in my heart and mind.

Fig and I considered adoption. We agreed that Miriam needed a sibling, so we contacted the Department of Social Services and filed the necessary papers.

It wasn't the only option we investigated. We also saw a fertility specialist who performed corrective surgery. I smiled on the inside when that French doctor shook my hand, and confidently predicted, "Mrs. Hamlin, you'll be pregnant in six months."

He had done all he, a mere man, could do, but I had just talked with the Creator of babies. My God had assured me we would have another child. But to my question, *Which way?* he answered, *"Don't ask, Susan, just trust me."*

From that point on I was free from monthly anxiety and grief. God had spoken, and I had chosen to believe him. Still, it was a huge surprise to receive the call, almost four years after applying for adoption, asking us to pick up our seven-week-old son at one p.m. the next day!

So, my little prince came, my long-prayed-for treasure, on June 29, 1979. I had no idea then of God's plan to use this precious little boy to make me cry uncle.

A little prince, huh? Well, he was in one sense, as he surely commanded the attention of these two adults. From the beginning, Nate would sweat in our cool house. He was constantly moving and couldn't sleep. Each late night I'd pat him and sing till I was dead on my feet. Yes, we let him cry, but after hours of letting him scream on several occasions, we gave up. Sometimes, we put him in his car seat, and drove around until he fell asleep. That worked, as long as we didn't jostle him on the way to bed.

Many a night, at a year old, I'd read to him, sing, and he'd close his eyes. I'd tip-toe out of the room, ready to fall into bed. As I stepped across the threshold of his door, I allowed myself to take a quick glance back. There he'd be, pushed up on his arms, his bright brown eyes watching me retreat with a look that said, *Where ya goin', Mom?*

Those were long days. His energy left both of us weary.

We sent Nate to a Christian school when he was five. Then, at six, his first grade teacher told me that he was bright but couldn't stay still at his desk. Therefore, he wasn't included in the top group of his class.

That year, Nate and his buddy in mischief, Brad, got caught trying to escape over the school's chain-link fence. Off the two of them went to the principal's office. Nate was first. When he came out, Brad giggled as Nate's downcast expression told him that his book-in-trousers plan had not worked. His buddy thought he would be tougher. Instead, Brad came from the principal boohooing. Nate loved to tell that story.

I was becoming more aware of the adventurous little limit-pusher we had, and was begging God to help me know how to both encourage and discipline him.

My mom loved her grandchildren, so she drove the six hours to visit us fairly often. Once, she and I corralled Nate for the chore of buying shoes. Mom never told me exactly what Nate had said to the salesman, but whatever it was, was inappropriate. She kindly pulled him aside.

"Nate, Grandmother will give you five dollars if you'll go back and say you're sorry to the salesman."

He didn't hesitate but answered her respectfully and clearly, "Grandmother, keep your five dollars. I'm not sorry, and I'm not going to say I am."

Nate had refreshing candor, even as a six-year-old.

3

Boy of the Jungle

In 1985 Fig quit his state job. We sold our house in
South Carolina, packed, and flew halfway around
the globe to Papua New Guinea to be linguist/trans-
lators with Wycliffe Bible Translators. Miriam was
eleven, Nate six. I hoped to homeschool the kids in
the village and wondered why more translators did
not do that.

I soon discovered that we were living in a very
different culture.

One night, some months after we'd arrived in the
village, the leader, Jems Nawi, came to visit. After
coughing a polite "I'm here" at the door, he came
in and began making small talk. He seemed to have
something important on his mind, and Fig and I
were on edge, wondering what we'd done.

Here's the short version of what he announced to
us: "Newton, we've decided which of our men is to
marry your daughter."

Yikes! We were floored, and in a flash, the boarding school at the mission center at Ukarumpa made sense. Jems went on to say that until Miriam married, she could not go out with her friends even to play or hunt food, as young men would see this as a come-on.

The next day, we were up early on the radio to schedule a plane to take her the four hours to the Center. She would be cared for by another mum and dad in one of the school's children's hostels there.

It was a painful separation as Miriam began her school schedule at Ukarumpa, which meant alternating between ten weeks there and two with us in the village. I sobbed as I considered losing my girl. But after a couple of days, I dried my eyes and gave my daughter over to God's safe keeping. I knew he could make this time away good for her, and I was willing to believe him.

Life went on for the three of us in the village.

Nate adapted quickly to the jungle. The Nai people are hunters and gatherers, and he became quite a village boy—a good hunter with bow and arrow, and able to catch anything that moved. One wet night he went tree-frogging with the villagers. They nabbed 168 frogs before midnight, two hundred more in the wee hours. He said matter-of-factly, "I ate thirty of them, but got a tummy ache from the slime."

There wasn't school for the village children, and the area under our house-on-stilts made a perfect playground for them. As you can imagine, Nate was very distracted and wondered why he was the unfortunate one who needed school. Many a day, after he finished his two hours of lessons, I would cry, asking myself what, if anything, he'd learned.

I was amazed, though, at how he quickly he blended into village activities. He learned the trade language, sounding very much like them, and assimilated to their ways of living. During our first few years there, bartering was how villagers did business with one another. With the young boys, Nate found his rubber bands were a desirable item. They braided them to make slingshots or wore them as ornamental bracelets. Trading these gave him a big name among the guys.

There was something else as common in the village as my boy's rubber bands, but very undesirable. Nate had about a dozen bouts of malaria, with its cycles of chills, fever, and sweats. Once, he was playing at the other end of the village when *Bam!*— sapping weakness overtook him. Nate recognized the symptom and immediately began the two-hundred-yard slog home. He slept most of the hours for three days, a break for his parents.

Nate had been diagnosed with ADHD before we went to PNG, and had trouble learning the way most kids do. Before that, I was one of those who pooh-poohed that diagnosis as an excuse for a child who simply needed more discipline to stay in his seat like the rest of the class. Uhhh, nope. It was obvious that Nate had something different going on. In the village, my student could do twenty math problems correctly one day, but the next morning he would stare blankly at the very same sort of question. He'd forgotten the whole process, and we had to start over.

Many a day I wondered how to help him. I prayed a lot for his schooling and whenever possible tried hands-on projects. I also helped him memorize poems, like Tennyson's "Charge of the Light Brigade." He liked the rhythm—and the fighting, of course. Although school was a struggle for him, each day God gave me strength to push through.

Fig read to us every night from famous works. Nate could retell every night's reading, with many details. He loved the *Lord of the Rings* trilogy, and after Fig read the last word of *The Return of the King*, he begged his dad to begin again.

Whenever we flew from the village to the Center, Nate went right into a regular classroom. It was never easy for him to fit in. He had the smarts, but teachers at Ukarumpa were uncertain how to respond to

Nate's different learning style. You mothers who have kids with learning disabilities know the deep hurt you feel when teachers don't understand your child and may unjustly accuse him of being lazy or trying to act dumb. The child actually does not remember his address and phone number and does, in fact, lose his place in the book. I remember Nate saying that when someone dropped a pencil, he was mesmerized as he watched it spin and roll until it stopped. He could think of nothing else, especially the book his class was reading aloud, with his turn coming. When your child suffers, you suffer, even more than he. You yearn for a solution. But in Nate's case, there didn't seem to be one.

Nate loved animals. Furthermore, he appreciated their abilities. He'd noticed many times that his cat turned its ears in different directions simultaneously, responding to different sounds. In fourth grade he decided to investigate this for his science project. He rigged strings through the kitchen and attached them to two objects. Activated with his foot, the objects tumbled at the same moment, and he took black-and-white photos of the cat's head. The pictures with captions earned him a good grade.

The teacher doubted that the project had originated with him. In that, she was wrong. But her mistake didn't keep me from being encouraged that Nate could succeed in some aspect of school.

Besides trouble with schoolwork, there were some social cues Nate didn't pick up on.

When he was with friends, he was constantly poking, hitting, or wrestling with them. Because of these behaviors, parents at the Center didn't always invite him to their kids' parties. Once, I stepped in. I knew the parents of the boy whose birthday it was. In fact, the father was one of Nate's favorite teachers. Mr. Nielson and his wife were very understanding people, so I called the mother, and asked her to let Nate come. She said he could.

That very evening Nate came home laughing and telling us about his friend Tim and their latest prank. They had gone after dark and TP'd every tree in a neighbor's yard while the family ate. (At the Center, streaming toilet paper from people's trees was the practical joke of choice. In fact, only the most liked folks had it done to them.) In his excitement, Nate's buddy had talked aloud while they worked, and out came the man of the house! He grabbed Tim from behind, while Nate blended in with a nearby tree. His friend, though, wasn't going to take the rap alone and pointed straight at Nate.

"Mom, it was a perfect TP job. They didn't know a thing until Tim forgot where he was. Now we have to be over there early in the morning to clean up the mess. Mr. Nielson is a great teacher, but he didn't appreciate our artwork."

Did you guess it? Nate had TP'd the folks throwing the party the next day. Ugh. I was a bit teary as I realized my best efforts to help Nate fit in had failed again. It was becoming clearer that I wasn't going to be able to rescue Nate. It just wasn't my job.

When he was in grade five, God continued loosening my grip on this precious treasure. It was the afternoon before Nate's first band concert. I was working on supper when he came to me pleading, "Mom, I can't play tonight. Give me private drum lessons, but I just can't play in front of these people. Please, Mom, don't make me do it."

I assured him everyone is nervous before his first concert, but he could do it. Nate was immovable. I needed a minute to be alone. I went to my room and cried out to God, *Lord, my brothers and I all played in the band. It's enriching to know and play music. Is it so wrong to want this good thing for Nate?*

God spoke to my heart, just like you'd talk to a friend. *"Susan,"* he gently answered, *"I know that band is good, but the issue is whether you insist on planning this boy's life, working out your own will and purposes for him. Or will you allow me to work out my plan?"*

"Well, if you put it that way, sure, I want to give him to you, Lord."

Nate, held less tightly, sat with us for the concert.

That same year, Nate's chorus teacher, Lee, came to our house on Center. When out of the village, our family attended the same Bible study with him and his wife. He knew that Nate had been having trouble, misbehaving in other classes, but he wanted us to know, "He didn't in mine." He continued with a smile, "It's also true that he hasn't sung a note the whole semester. So, I wonder, may he sit out the concert tonight?"

Nate's resolve not to be disruptive in Lee's class really spoke to me of his character. He liked this teacher, and he acted like it. This was another clue that God himself would need to mold this son of mine. Only he had the perfect design for Nate's life—and the power to execute it.

Looking back, I thank God for the glimpses of his goodness I saw as I trusted him. I was discovering that the more I trusted, the more I was convinced of his trustworthiness.

4

Wanna Go Home

When Nate was thirteen, shortly after Miriam had left PNG for college in the States, he began talking about wanting to go home. It seemed a sudden desire, and I thought it might simply be missing his sister and would ease with time. That didn't happen.

Instead, one afternoon he came home from school upset, repeating his plea, "I wanna go home!" He stomped off to his room, slammed the door, locked it, and emptied all his drawers, making a pile in the middle of the floor. Hearing the commotion, we asked him to let us in so we could talk. He didn't respond, so we jimmied the lock.

There he was, splay-legged at the bottom of a mountain of clothes and boyhood treasures, tearing up his cherished comics one by one.

The Christian psychologist at the Center counseled us the next day, "You must take him back to the U.S. This time he acted out in your home. Next time, he'll act out on Center, and the Administration will make you go home. I've seen too many of these situations."

Right away we began booking flights and sent a message to our translator in the village that the language program would be on hold. We said quick good-byes and were on a plane within days. Our friends packed up our house and put our gear into a storage shed after we left.

That was not what we had planned. This little treasure of ours was causing us to leave the translation project, and we had no way of knowing how long fixing Nate would take. I remember hoping we could go home, give him a couple of years there, spend time with his sister, reconnect with his friends, and return to PNG. Our psychologist friend knew better and set us straight.

"You might be thinking you'll pick up a Band-Aid for Nate, then return to PNG. Think again. This problem will not go away quickly."

He was right. We would have five and a half turbulent years during which I wondered not only if we would return to PNG, but even if our family would survive.

The three of us flew halfway around the world to the Wycliffe Center in North Carolina. There were counseling and health care for missionaries available, and we'd be with some friends and with others like us, back from the field.

It was the first of January 1993. The night was dark, rainy, and miserable. Key in hand, we entered an empty house. I'm sure our jet lag and the sudden switch from Southern Hemisphere summer to Northern Hemisphere winter added to the feeling that we'd been dropped in the middle of nowhere. We knew this was supposed to be the U.S., but there was no TV and little food in the fridge.

Nate was still out of sorts, doubting that this was the pasture that had looked so green from afar. I guessed his thoughts because I, too, was skeptical. Where would Nate go to school? Could he make it in a regular classroom? And more to the point, could we make it through the night?

I felt as gloomy as the weather. He broke the silence with his old refrain, "Mom, I said I want to go home. This isn't home." Without a clear voice from heaven, we changed plans.

That next morning, we packed our gear in the truck and headed south, not knowing where we would live but knowing that we were now taking Nate home, where our old church family and friends awaited us.

Then why did I feel as if we were on a runaway stagecoach, gathering speed, with the reins flapping in the wind?

Middle school is not the ideal time for a child to begin at a new school. Think about it. Nate was used to roaming the jungle after two hours of homeschool in the village. Or, at the Center, he went to school with translator kids and a few village kids from the surrounding language groups. His best friend was one of those from the nearby village. Those classmates had similar experiences of a third world country. But here, Nate was attending a five-star, all-American school.

I shouldn't be surprised that I've hunted in vain for my journals from these stormy adolescent years. They don't exist. I simply didn't have the energy, or the heart, at the end of each day to put pen to paper. My memory, however, has many permanent impressions.

Shortly after we arrived back in South Carolina, I took Nate to our family doctor. He informed me that Nate was self-medicating with marijuana for his depression. He prescribed an antidepressant instead. It helped, but Nate was especially sensitive to the side effects and used it for only a few months.

By the time he was fourteen, cigarettes, marijuana, and alcohol were Nate's meds to calm himself and lighten his dark, depressed world. At night he made a fire in our backyard. I had seen it only once, but he told me later that it was an every-night affair, after we hit the sack.

Nate had two neighborhood fellows he liked, but I cut them off due to the one's drug use and the other's smart mouth. Nate found others, though, and many a weekend night he called from some way-out place asking for a ride home. I'd find him standing in the dark, alone, beside the road.

He was also getting more uncooperative about our rules, and I knew something had to give.

Things weren't going well at school either. Although it had a top rating, the school wasn't made for the likes of Nate. He began committing all sorts of school misdemeanors. One of his demerits was for lying down in a body-size depression in the schoolyard and lighting a cigarette! Really, Nate? Like he was stalking prey, my jungle boy was trying to remain unseen.

There were times when Nate would open up and share his heart with me. Riding in the car somehow calmed him, and he would talk. I often took advantage of this quieting effect. Occasionally, he teared as he talked, and I saw his tenderness, and his desire to act differently.

5

Scary Times

There were also horrific times. One night, when Fig was working to midnight, I checked to make sure Nate was in his room so I could close up the house and finally get to sleep. I knocked on his door several times. No answer. I went in, saw an empty bed and wide-open window. When I stuck my head out, there was a body lying in the shadow of the house.

"Nate!" I cried.

No response sent me running in a panic out the kitchen door and into the back yard. I bent over him and heard him breathing. I shook him, saw him open his eyes. I sternly told him to get to bed. My heart wanted to hug him; my hands, to strangle him. That was thirty-two years ago.

Another frightening afternoon, I picked Nate up from school. He was in a terrible mood, and when I said something—don't remember what—about him using marijuana, he became enraged. He grabbed his windshield visor as if to rip it off.

I knew I needed to get somewhere safe soon, so I pulled over immediately into a gas station, put on the emergency brake, grabbed my keys, and hurried inside. I went straight to the cashier, asked to use her phone, and called the police.

As I waited for an officer to come, I sat in a booth. Nate plopped down, facing me. As he continued his tirade, his voice suddenly changed. He got right in my face and proceeded to tell me how he was going to take his index finger, which he held even closer, and gouge out my eye from its socket.

As Nate's voice uttered this awful thing, I saw his eyes turn a dazzling green! I had never witnessed anything like it before, nor have I since.

Just then the policeman arrived and asked me what was wrong. I saw Nate's shoulders relax, his back straighten, and his face go from a fiendish scowl to the sweetest demeanor. He had his own voice again and offered softly, "Sir, I don't know why Mom called you, but I think everything is fine."

The policeman turned and looked at me as if I were the problem. I assured him that everything was *not* fine. We were just blocks from home, and I told the officer I did not want Nate to follow me. I was shaken, but I faced my son and told him that he needed to find somewhere else to sleep for the night. My only offer was the open carport.

As I think again about this scary event, I realize that Satan wanted to terrify me, make me think more about the Enemy, and less about God's powerful care and protection of Nate. The Enemy's scheme was to shake my faith. Instead, that shaking strengthened me, reminding me of the Lord of Hosts who himself was fighting for my son.

We moms have been given the task to watch over our children, to know where they are and whom they're with. But ultimately, God is the only one who can protect them from the Enemy. He wants us to entrust these prodigals to him, pray for them, and not be afraid, not even in very frightening times (Psalm 46:1–3, 6–7).

As things went from bad to worse in Nate's life, I kept in touch with his teachers, and they, too, were out of answers. Finally, the school said, "Enough." The last count of his demerits was 192 (which Nate kept in a shoebox), too many for this five-star school, and in 1994 he was expelled at age fifteen.

This was a blow to us, and we wondered what to do with him. I had thought about homeschooling, but Fig immediately vetoed that. Nate wasn't obeying basic rules or listening to us in general, so why would he listen to me as his teacher? We needed to find a school, and soon, because we had this active, uncommunicative, defiant teen at home 24-7!

There was an Opportunity School nearby, where students who couldn't make it in a regular classroom could finish high school. They took both day pupils and boarders. It wasn't my choice, but God seemed to be leading us to put Nate there as a day student.

After a few weeks of Nate attending this new school, I went to see the principal. I wanted this woman to know Nate's background, and show her that his parents are concerned about him. After recounting a bit of Nate's life in the jungle of Papua New Guinea, this very masculine woman responded with, "Mrs. Hamlin, Nate's the youngest student here, and he is our baby. He's so respectful, and we care about him."

I burst into tears. I was so concerned about Nate's protection in a school full of bigger guys. The Enemy kept whispering, *God will not deliver him.* I surely had no way to keep him safe . . . but God did. I had relaxed my hold on this precious treasure, and God had put a shield around him (Psalm 3:2–3). I had every reason to keep trusting him fully for Nate's care.

Outside school, Nate began staying out way past curfew and became very belligerent with us. After giving him many chances to remain a day student and obey our house rules, we finally boarded him there. With doorless rooms, the staff tried to keep an eye on everyone. The bathroom was an exception and became a playground for bullies. Nate said that when the weaker boys came in, they were ambushed and told to empty their pockets.

Later, after several successful weekends back at home with us and obeying our rules, Nate was allowed to be a day student again. It was only temporary. Teachers saw him arrive on campus with a clear head, only to be high as a kite by first period. He had told us that he could get drugs or alcohol on campus. The administration couldn't have this happening, as it reflected badly on them. They summoned us to meet. Besides pointing out Nate's addictions, they offered him rehab. Already high that morning, he responded, "I'm not ready." So they expelled him.

We were at another crossroad, clueless where to go next. In South Carolina one can't put a child out of the house until his eighteenth birthday. Fig and I loved our son, but we didn't love that he was using our home as a motel, not always coming home at night. As his mother, I couldn't just turn off my mother radar and go to sleep when it was late but he was still out. Nate kept choosing to break our very basic house rules. Also, he became destructive in his rages. Nine doors had fist holes. And I finally tired of his bad language, especially when directed at his dad.

I can picture the chair where he sat when I said, "Son, there is only one king of this house, and it's your dad. It's time you go build your own kingdom."

Nate knew it meant he'd be out on his own, and he begged me to let him stay. He pressed me by saying that he knew he'd have to let people flop at any place he had, which would eventually get him into trouble. He added, "And I'll probably end up in jail."

I told him he might be self-prophesying, but only he had the power to make choices that would confirm or avoid his predictions. Oh, how my mother heart ached, though I knew this was right and God was near (Psalm 46:1).

Within a month, and with a job and money to pay the rent, Nate moved into a trailer and was on his own. Time passed, and we heard that he, along with others, had been arrested for breaking into someone's backyard shed. When the police went to arrest him at his trailer, they found a fugitive living there, someone with a warrant in Virginia. This was Nate's first arrest, and it fulfilled almost exactly what he had predicted.

Do I ever wonder if things would have been different had I let Nate stay home? Sure, I have had those thoughts, but I can't go back. I can give all those decisions to God, both the ones that ended well, and those that appear to have ended badly.

I could also have taken some blame for Nate's lawlessness, feeling guilt and shame, as if this were my fault. He had to face the consequences of his own bad decisions. These would be the levers that would inch our son closer to God. As a parent I had done my duties. I had bathed that boy in prayer, and had given him into God's hands. What does it matter that I had never imagined my little prince being in jail, or me, his mom, having to stand in line with others visiting their relatives? Yes, it was humbling, but I was developing fellow-feeling and compassion for these other poor and needy folks. There's lots of good in that.

I asked Nate recently how bad it was in the Opportunity School with the older boys.

"I liked that school," he told me. "It was good. I know it was the only option I had. I was about to get expelled from my second middle school, but it was like, if you leave now for Opportunity School, then you can leave without being expelled. That's how it was explained to me. You didn't throw me to the lions. Yeah, there were some tough boys that bullied younger guys. But you grow up anyway. I didn't have to worry about that too much."

He added, "The teachers helped you pass. What it was, they'd make you do just two or three of the problems on your own. It's like they're not trying to hold you back. That education that they have, if you're not good at it, if you're not excelling in it, then you're not going to be doing that as a job. You know what I mean? So why try to learn it and struggle through it?"

I was so glad to get Nate's view of a place where I had been so reluctant to put him. God had led, and I got to hear that something positive resulted from my obedience.

Moms, when the Enemy of our souls, the devil, comes around to discourage you as you look back on some hard decisions you had to make, don't let him burden you with guilt. God has said that he is working to make everything, both good and bad, turn to your good and to the good of your child, when you love him (Romans 8:28). He—the almighty God—loves you; he offers forgiveness. Trust his Word, and tell the devil to leave you alone, in the name of Jesus (James 4:7).

6

Help from the Hills

In May 1995, when Nate was sixteen, we were in the Pocono Mountains for family counseling. One afternoon, he was off exploring, and came upon a woodchuck.

"Mom, I saw him in the cornfield, and began running after him. We'd weave in and out of the rows, and get so tired that we'd both stop, each of us gasping for air. I'd look up and find him looking straight at me as if to say, 'Ready? Let's go,' and we'd start again."

That night, I was speechless, and rattled, as Nate sat watching TV with this wild animal curled up in his lap. What was I to do?

At some point that evening, the woodchuck nipped him. As there had been some cases of rabies in the area, we called the Department of Health. They said they needed to test the animal and would have to kill him to do it.

This chuck was only one of Nate's wild animal casualties. The groundhog had been a real catch for him, but the authorities said it had to die. Mother and son both wondered why.

Well, it happened again. Later, while visiting Fig's family in North Carolina, Nate used a short stick and a bare hand to catch a mature rattlesnake on his uncle Joe's land. Nate had previously sold a black widow spider and her eggs at the local Saturday flea market, and hoped he could sell his rattler there. He brought it to the house in a small cooler he'd found. The sound that snake made! He proudly showed his find to Fig's dad, and before we could intervene, we were grieving another loss. His Geepop decreed that Nate had no use for something so dangerous, and, without debate, cut off its head.

These losses left Nate hurting and confused. He was finding it hard to fit into this regular world in the United States. Neither his wild animals nor his own wild nature could find a place.

Nate had been trained by his years of experiences in Papua New Guinea. How could he live in this so-called civilized environment, when exploring the woods, building fires, and living in the freedom of nature was what he loved?

One of the most terrifying times for me, as his mom, occurred during that same few days in the Poconos, at the Tuscarora Resource Center.

For months, Nate had been huffing butane, gasoline, Wite-Out, anything volatile. These solvents can cause permanent brain damage. I was so afraid he might lose his sharp mind, or die. After a few counseling sessions, it became obvious that the psychologists were touching sensitive areas in Nate's heart, because each day he needed to huff more and more to dull his pain. He had stashes of gas all around campus.

My self-appointed mission was to see where he went to get high and empty the container. You can imagine how stressful this was, as I tried desperately to save him.

One evening, Nate locked himself in a barn full of lawn equipment. We could see him through a crack in the door as he went from mower to edger to gas can, reeling, in a drunken near-stupor, yelling out oaths and curses.

As I watched, I softly cried, thinking how deep his agony must be to resort to such a mind-numbing substance. I felt that the evening was a perfect picture of my life with this son: I was watching, locked out, totally unable to keep him from destruction. Gratefully, the staff came quickly, broke the latch, and took Nate out. He was so fired up that it took several men to restrain him. He finally calmed down, and we went back to our cabin.

Out of that counseling, Nate somehow was delivered from huffing, and for a time after we returned to South Carolina, he stayed clean of any substance. It was a needed time of refreshment for him—and for me.

Unfortunately, because of privacy laws, the counselors couldn't tell us anything they had learned from the sessions. I wondered what problems Nate had dealt with, and how long this freedom might last.

7

Will We Two Survive?

Boy, am I ever glad someone told me early on, as Nate began to rebel, that Fig and I needed to guard our relationship. They said that the hard-case teen almost always makes it through these tough years, but many marriages do not.

Why is a defiant teen so hard on a marriage? Well, he does not have a broken bone that can be set, and heal in six weeks. He does not have the flu, responsive to an antiviral drug or liquids and pain relievers. The trouble a hurting teen has cannot be ended by some treatment. It is a stage he must pass through, and it often takes a long time. Many days I was so tired of giving reasons for our rules, for what I was asking him to do, or waiting for him to come home, or wondering where he was and what he was doing. Nothing was quick obedience, and I mean nothing.

With Nate, it was either long talks late at night, or no talk at all. Most evenings I was beat, and had little desire even to chat with my hubby, much less engage in anything amorous. Fig and I did keep our monthly date nights, with only one rule—no talking about kids. Looking at Fig across a meal that someone else had cooked, and seeing him relaxed, and quite attractive, fueled my empty tank and gave me a needed spark.

Besides the excitement and humdrum of any close relationship, a marriage is tested because of the differences between men and women, dads and moms. Yes, God made parents to be male and female, and this works well most days in a normal setting. But if there's an angry or sullen teen questioning all rules, and breaking every one of them, Mom and Dad are in a pressure cooker, and will react differently. In general, a dad is concerned about his teen becoming a responsible person. A mom is more interested in caring for her child and tending to his emotional well-being.

Fig saw it like this: "A man doesn't come into marriage knowing how his wife will respond as a mother. When difficulties squeeze her, what he sees will often surprise and disconcert him. She likely appears not to be on his side. So, added to conflicts with the kid, he's in conflict with his wife."

As for me, I felt like a full-time referee. I was pulled both ways, always in the middle. I am both a wife and a mom. So, whenever we disagreed concerning how to deal with Nate's rebellion, Fig thought I had jumped ship. Actually, I was trying to keep the ship afloat. Many a day, when my two men were at it, I strongly wished they could go out back, put on the gloves, and duke it out. But even the laws of thirty years ago did not permit it.

Besides disobedience, Nate called his dad every ugly name he could think of. I hated that for Fig. When the time was right, I told Nate he was going to regret those words. He did regret them, and he later wrote his dad just that.

Fig and I saw our situation grow worse, more intense, with only occasional and brief lulls in the storm. I'll answer your question right up front. Did you pray? Yes, I prayed. Did your husband pray? Yes, he prayed. (He says he fumed at least as much as he prayed.) Did you pray together? Yes, some. But unlike some other times when I'd prayed, this trouble did not end.

I urge you wives to pray especially for your husband during this gut-wrenching time. Be patient with him. He is the head of the family. Fig said, "When a dad is stripped of solutions, the deepest, the permanent, the irreconcilable, the frustrating, and maddening differences between a dad and a mom are most obvious."

Trouble in the family means to the man that he has failed. This perceived failure made Fig angry and resentful. He said he needed help, then described his fears in these unspoken words: [He] *imagined that the fix would require a single, simple, crushing spiritual decision that would somehow make him less angry, more tolerant of disobedience, and more hopeful while Nate's irrational behavior raged. This dad could see no way he could pull that off.* Because of his fear, we did not get much family counseling. Fig thought this situation was black and white—white for others, black for him. That's how he described it. But counseling could have been a great help.

Even in our ignorance, I will say that God was gracious. There were times when I felt Fig was reacting to some infraction of Nate's too severely. I heard Satan's whispers that such a strong response could discourage Nate so deeply that he would not recover. I was reminded, though, of Paul's command for wives in Ephesians 5:22. So, by faith I submitted, and held my breath until the shoe dropped. But it did not drop.

In fact, the more I obeyed Paul's instructions, the more I realized that reaching out to this dad and mom, there stood my heavenly Father. There were three of us holding up Nate, not just two. We were bound to make it through.

8

Sister and Brother

Recently, I was asked how Miriam dealt with her brother, the one who caused such confusion and upheaval in our family life. I felt guilty about not having asked that question myself. It is natural that the child who screams the loudest gets the attention. That was Nate.

But it was poignant, in mid-2024, as Fig and I listened to our daughter's reply to that question. Instead of trauma, she recalled with a hardy laugh a bareback ride with Nate at Ukarumpa about thirty-five years before. He was seated up front when the horse decided to trot. Up and down, up and down they went as Miriam tried unsuccessfully to get Begum to canter. Instead, the horse abruptly halted, throwing both riders off, toppling Miriam onto her brother, whose head was on a rock in the road. Ouch!

She referred only to the good times, saying she's not one to live in the past. True, we had blessed, whole, and sunny seasons in our family life. For example, thirty times we walked the eight hours to and from our village, stopping to let Fig shed his sixty-pound pack. We cooled off in a mountain pool and gulped the pure water, washing down beef biscuits, in glorious shade. Miriam said those treks, and the freedom she felt, inspired her love for walking. "I'm forever grateful," she added.

At the Center, in the PNG highlands, brother and sister rode horses and enjoyed their myriad pets—guinea pigs, cats, a champion dog, a green tree python, a lorikeet, and Nate's tawny Papuan frogmouth owl and brahminy kite, both of which he hand-fed daily.

Children grow up, and Miriam graduated from Ukarumpa High School in June 1992. The new graduate went to the U.S. for more schooling. She found pretty quickly that college was not for her, but wanted to work instead.

It was after only six months that Nate trashed his room at Ukarumpa, insisted that he must go home, and we left PNG. Soon after that, Miriam landed her job, moved back in with us, and we were a family again. But it was not the same happy family. Nate was controlled by drugs and alcohol, and we three were held captive by his tyrannical rule for over five years.

As Miriam observed, "We were just trying to survive."

At the end of those terrible years, 1993 to 1998, Nate was in jail a second or third time. He took the blame for his actions, expressed true sorrow for keeping us from our job overseas, and urged us, "Mom, please go back to your work." Nate's statement confirmed God's leading of us to leave him on his own. We were soon off to continue the translation program in Papua New Guinea.

But how did Miriam (age twenty-four) deal with Nate (age nineteen) during the next four years (1998–'02) when we were gone? She had to handle a very unpredictable, needy brother who was in and out of jail. She did have work, was in a solid church, and had friends. Shortly after we'd left her, our long-time friends, her substitute parents, bless them, found a home for her. Miriam spoke of her short, narrow one-bedroom trailer, with trees and a fenced-in yard for her dog, Ranger, as "not the Taj Mahal, but my own place." The negative side of her having a home was that Nate wanted to share it.

The story of our two in the U.S., with parents ten thousand miles away, can best be seen through a few hand-picked emails from her and letters from Nate from jail.

From Nate

January 25, 1998 — I got your letter today and I want to thank you very much for it. I just want to say that I am very, very sorry for all the things I've done to you and to God. I'm forced to think about it every day. I want you to know that you and Dad have done everything for me and will continue to. I want you to know that no other parents would have had the patience or the love and goodness that you do. Nobody being a Christian has the quality you all do. I could have never have made it and never can make it without you all beside me. And I never could have made it if my parents and sister were anybody else, Christian or not. One day we'll do something as a family. Nate

From Miriam

September 1998 — Haven't gotten my visitation requests back to see Nate, but will keep you up to date on how that goes. I can't wait to see him face to face.

September 22, 1998 — I love and miss you guys. When I got home from work today, I *had a note from Nate. He graduated from one correctional institution and is going to another. On the same day he graduated, he also got his GED. Know that's one thing we've been praying for, and Nate did sound happy. I will be able to visit him on certain days, which are determined by alphabetical order.*

April 30, 1999 — Talked to Nate a couple of nights ago, and he is not getting out this weekend. The guy he was to work for and half live with said that he does not want Nate to live with them. So he's had to go and find another address to put on his release forms. Said he was giving them two halfway house numbers, one here and one in another town. Praise the Lord! Mum, we had one of the best conversations ever. Said we were both adults, and darn it, we should talk like it. Amen to that! I flat out told him that I was scared about him getting out, and he totally understood and said he would try his best to encourage me and all that. Says he's really changed and wants to more as time goes on. Talked for quite a while, not sure why the phone didn't cut off after fifteen minutes, but it didn't. I love and miss you bunches. Miriam

August 24, 1999 — Nate called raising Cain about "family" (me) not taking him in, but there is no way, and so many people have applauded me for making this decision up front with him. Mr. C told me during prayer time at home groups how proud he was of me and how I'm handling the Nate situation. That's nice to hear. Miriam

From Nate

December 21, 1999 — When I got locked up, the hearing officer recommended my release if I had a stable residence. They, in other words, would release me to a parole officer, so I called Miriam and said that I would stop drinking but just needed a place to stay at the most for three weeks and would have a job and pay her some rent. She said, "Oh no," all snappy like she does. I said that right now she was the only person that could give me my freedom. It just seems like even though I'm improving myself, she's not trying to work with me. I feel like she's totally disowned me. This is what's troubling me now.

I'm so sorry that I let things go the way they did back in the day. I was in such torment back then on drugs, with nothing to do but drugs. I was into the wrongest [sic] kind of things. When I got out of hand, I always had an excuse, like when I was real hard on y'all, I would think, "well, when I get through this phase and older, I'm gonna be extra nice to y'all and make up for everything." I just didn't realize or probably care that some things you can't ever fully make up for. I'll write y'all again when I get another of these aerograms. I love y'all. Nate

From Miriam

March 2, 2000 — Hey, I forgot to email you yesterday about the call I get from Nater. He called Friday before I left on my trip, and we had such a good chat. He did get my visitation form, and R and I can go as well as the grandparents. He seems to be doing well, and says he's just laying low so as to get out in the near future. Not sure when that is though. I told him about you all and just filled him in on what is going on here with me. Miriam

From Nate to his grandmother

July 6, 2000 — I got your letter a week ago and real happy to hear from you and to know that everything is good. As you probably know, I'm taking a welding course. I'm doing good in that, and if I can learn enough by the time I get out, I will pursue that jobwise. I've also been able to stop smoking for a month and about a week now. I hope that's the end of smoking. Well, I hardly ever write anybody because nothing new happens, so there's nothing to talk about. I love you and miss you so much. Nate

(Nate got out of jail sometime mid-2000 and was able to get a place to live and find a job.)

From Miriam

February 22, 2001 — Nate is doing great. He got another job right down the street from where his is now, making nine dollars an hour and doing strictly welding. K got him the job and has stopped by a couple of times to see how things are going. He's had a cold or something of the sort, went away, then I stopped by Saturday night, and he was still feeling a bit rough. He's been drinking a ton of OJ, and C *has bought him some eggs and more OJ, which I will take over tonight after prayer meeting. K also took him to Walmart and got him some jeans, gloves, and T-shirts for his job. He's kept up with his money quite well; now he gets paid every two weeks so will be giving me $200 (to hold) when I pick it up. His next meeting with his parole officer is March 5; he wants Ms. P to come and get him. Has been driving my car a bit and doing okay. Might take him next week for his permit.*

I'm doing well, work as steady as it always is. I've still been hanging out with the singles group at church and having a blast. With ever so much love, Miriam.

9

MERCY, the Promise

At the end of those four years of Miriam and Nate being on their own is when the tragedy of the stabbing occurred.

We had no idea whom to hire as a lawyer for Nate's case. In the past, we'd felt that if he'd done the deed, he could use a public defender to represent him. This time the charges were so serious, and the penalty potentially so severe, that it seemed he shouldn't wait in line for a PD. We needed a lawyer experienced in trying felony cases.

Most days I had to pinch myself to sense that all this was actually happening. The reality of Nate's overreacting and killing a man threw me hard on Jesus. Shortly after the tragic day, I was on my knees pleading with God to work through our defense attorney and the judge to give our son a fair ruling and sentence. As he often does, when I earnestly ask him for guidance, God spoke very plainly to me,

"*Susan, I will give Nate* mercy." I believed him and stored the promise away.

Nate's lawyer took several months to investigate the case. All the while, we had people around the world praying for us. When we heard that the lawyer was settling for a plea deal instead of a trial, we began praying for the right date so we would get the best judge.

Miriam, Fig, and I planned to be there, as our lawyer said we'd have a chance to say something to the judge before sentencing. When it was time to speak, Fig and I both stood and spoke. I can't recall much of what we said. I do remember I told the judge that Nate had lived from age six to thirteen with people in the jungle of Papua New Guinea who believed the highest value was protecting those in their family and community.

The judge then gave the sentence, "Nathaniel Oliver Hamlin, I sentence you to fourteen years, without parole, to be served . . ." And the gavel fell.

I heard it plainly: fourteen years! *Lord, you said you'd give Nate mercy. That's mercy?* I left the courtroom in a daze. Someone guided me to a side room where I briefly hugged my son, reminded him I loved him, and said good-bye. Our dear pastor was with us, and as we walked out, he explained that this judge was up for reelection, perhaps the reason for the excessive sentence.

That night, when alone with God, I cried out my question again, "You said you'd give Nate mercy. Fourteen years surely doesn't sound like it."

God was there, and I heard him ask kindly, *"Susan, will you trust me with what seems like a cruel sentence?"*

I knew right away that trusting God's Word was my best option. "Yes, Father, if you'll help me, I'll believe this sentence is mercy." And the deal was struck.

Below is a letter from Nate in prison, 2003, shortly after we left the U.S.

Dear Mom and Dad,

I really don't know what to say but that I feel good about the plea. And I'm sure that it's the best thing and the right thing. I think y'all feel the same way. I had ordered you a Mother's Day card, but I couldn't get it. Happy Mother's Day, though. I hope you didn't cry or make a scene, but it really doesn't matter what people think anymore. You're so much better than anybody's parents in here. Most of them will lie, and more, on the stand. And if they don't like it, they can always come talk to me about it. I started smoking Monday because of court, but you can't smoke in R&E [where inmates are given mental health evaluations], so I'll be quitting by the time I get to the camp.

I can get at least a job in the kitchen if there's an opening, and try to gain some weight, and finally get to go outside. I heard the food will be better. I called about 12:00 a.m. Miriam answered had a pretty good talk, but it wasn't long enough. That's the only time they'll let me call.

I'm glad y'all can finally get back to your life's work. I wish I could have not been so selfish, enough to let you go years ago. I'm sorry. I can't tell you how sorry I am. I want you to tell people if they ask how I am that I have done it all, and I'm paying for it. Nobody should have to go through some of the things I went through to say I've done it all. All the depressing thoughts, stress, guilt, shame, sorrow, side effects, and thinking what I could have been and if I hadn't done this or done that instead.

The drugs just weren't worth it, and the consequences are lifelong, not like this little nothing bit of time I got here. I have learned patience and what drugs do when you're not high and when you are.

I don't want anybody there messing up like that because for one thing I can't name anyone except maybe Dalton Nawi [a PNG friend of Nate's] that could have survived what I've been through. And if he could, he would have to harden his thoughts and conscience and heart.

But what I discovered was after all that, all you get is a short temper ready to snap at almost anything. I discovered you can still have heart even if you don't do drugs, and you're better off without the side effects of drugs and the viscious [sic] mind-set. I wish I had done it that way, but I've made improvements.

After the first four months here I've only gone off maybe two or three times, which is really good for in here. I'm thankful for that because if I'd still been on drugs within ten years, I probably would have killed someone or gotten killed just because I had to do it, all not realizing what kind of control it would have on the spur of the moment on me. But I see all that now.

And I'm changing. I don't look for trouble anymore. I think I've got a better personality because I haven't been ready and down for whatever plotting of violence and I feel good about it. It's easier to deal with people and problems. I can't believe how much Ganna [Fig's mom] has written me. I so hope she gets better. She deserves it. Please tell Uncle Pete I said, "Hey," and I appreciate his note. It said it all. And please thank everybody for me. And thank you for being there for me, not just in court. I love y'all and will write when I get to R&E.

—Nate

10

Words of Life

In 2000, two years before the stabbing, I read 2 Chronicles 20:1–30 and wrote about its impact on me in my journal.

Jehoshaphat, King of Judah, was facing a mighty army and cried out to God in desperation, "For we have no power to face this vast army that is attacking us. We do not know what to do, but our eyes are upon you" (2 Chronicles 20:12).

I was hardly able to bear the pain of seeing my son self-destruct, and surely unable to reach in and change his heart. Like that vast army facing Jehoshaphat, Nate had problems far too big for me.

God's Spirit urged me to follow this king's example, and to keep my eyes on God wielding his saving power. Led by that same Spirit, Jahaziel, the priest, exhorted the people, "Do not be afraid or discouraged because of this vast army. For the battle is not yours, but God's" (2 Chronicles 20:15). And

Jahaziel continues in verse 17, "You will not have to fight this battle."

God spoke straight to my heart twenty-five years ago, *"Susan, this fight for Nate's full surrender is my battle; it's just between him and me. I have taken this fight out of your hands. I am the Lord, and the battle is mine."*

Such peace and deep gratitude flooded my heart as I felt that heavy burden for my son's deliverance fall away that day.

After God assured me that he would do the heavy lifting in the spiritual fight involving Nate, he then showed me my part. (Yes, we always have a part.) "Take up your positions" (2 Chronicles 20:17). *"I want you to take your position as my daughter, Fig's wife, and Nate's mom, and in that order. Depend on me to help you fulfill each role by the strength I give."*

That's his command, his chosen place for me. I'm Nate's mom, not his God. I can take my position as one who loves him, and pray. The deliverance of our wayward child is something that God will do in his time, and in his way. He has a plan. My part is to ask him to work. His part is to answer (Psalm 33:10–11).

Free now from paralyzing worry and fear, I can live the productive life God has designed for me.

Jahaziel also urged the people to "stand firm" (2 Chronicles 20:17). One doesn't know what the God of the universe has in mind for your son or daughter. Be prepared to wait. This historical battle was fought over days. God's battle for your willful child will take longer, probably a great while longer. You can choose a shortcut, and usurp the Commander's part, but it won't be God's ways, and won't have God's perfect ending.

Don't lose faith and abandon ship when you see nothing but bad happening. God is not a man who can lie (Numbers 23:19).

The last order to the people was to "see the deliverance the LORD will give you" (2 Chronicles 20:17).

We moms are made to keep an eye on our youngsters. It's what we should do. God's Word at the same time urges us to "fix our eyes on Jesus, the pioneer and perfecter of faith. For the joy set before him he endured the cross, scorning its shame, and sat down at the right hand of the throne of God" (Hebrews 12:2). How does one do both at once?

When our charge is following a foolish and dangerous course, we see it and we panic. We forget that we're not seeing the whole story. God is fighting for that one. Sure, we don't shirk our parental duties and just look the other way, but by faith we focus our thoughts on Jesus, both who he is and what he's promised.

He promised to fight this battle for your loved one. So in prayer we join with him as he pushes back the Enemy, taking land in our rebel's heart, bit by bit, for his rule. And when there's no evidence of this happening, that's alright. We keep our eyes fixed. Deliverance is on the way.

God was so good to speak such life-changing truth to me those many years ago. That is because he is a communicator. He loves his creatures (you and me) and talks through a book (the Bible). My mom loved God's Word and started me memorizing Scripture early on. Those well-known verses, coupled with reading the Word each morning, keep me in touch with what the Lord has for me each day. I can keep my eyes on him and not cave to the enemies of fear and worry.

A favorite that Mom sang, and she sang throughout the day whether or not she got all the words right, was "Turn Your Eyes upon Jesus":

Oh soul, are you weary and troubled?
No light in the darkness you see?
There's light for a look at the Savior,
And life more abundant and free!
Turn your eyes upon Jesus,

Look full in his wonderful face,
And the things of earth will grow strangely dim,
In the light of his glory and grace.

This familiar chorus declares that looking at who Jesus is will change our perception of the problems we're facing. We learn that God loves us (Psalm 103:11), protects us (Psalm 3:3), and promises never to leave or forsake us (Hebrews 13:5). He also is able to and will "[foil] the plans of the nations . . . thwart the purposes of the peoples" (Psalm 33:10). We can take a seat and rest. His plans and purposes will "stand firm . . . through all generations" (Psalm 33:11).

This ballast of the Bible's life-giving truths will stabilize us, keeping us upright in these inevitable storms.

As we stand and look up to Jesus, we then "see the incredible rescue operation God will perform for [us—and our loved one]" (2 Chronicles 20:17 TLB).

Right beside my Bible I keep books that I read and reread. They were written by godly moms and dads who have had wandering children. *Prodigals and Those Who Love Them* by Ruth Bell Graham, *Rebel with a Cause* by Franklin Graham, *Come Back, Barbara*, by C. John Miller and Barbara Miller Juliani, and *Lena* by Margaret Jensen. When I'm being threatened by fear and confusion, hearing of another instance of my son's suffering, I refer to Scripture right away and am given hope to go on. But like a doughnut with coffee, these eyewitness testimonies add sweetness to the strong stuff of God's Word.

Moms, taking God at his word will be challenged. Satan knows when we are downhearted, when we compare our situation with our friend's, and when we otherwise become vulnerable to his lies. When that happens, stop and review what the Lord has said to you in his Word. Ask the Holy Spirit to refresh your heart with these truths. It's like tightening one's armor, making certain that those darts of the Enemy fall to the ground like straw.

II

Saved

How can a mom know what's in the heart of her child? Does his going down front during an altar call, or his desire to be baptized prove that he is a believer in Jesus Christ, that he has had his sins forgiven? God's Word says that we cannot know the thoughts of another. Yes, there must be good fruit, good actions, and a change from old ways when one turns to Jesus, but to what degree?

Nate had been in prison for six years when I received a letter I cherish. It will be one of the last treasures I part with! We were at the Ukarumpa Center in June 2009, and I received both a letter and a Mother's Day card from him. Reading the letter, I thought Nate sounded different somehow. I opened his card and read this message:

To simply the Best! There's no one like my Mother. No one can ever take your place or ever come close. Have a Happy Mother's Day, I love you so much and can't wait to see you. Thought you might want to know, I've finally accepted Jesus Christ thanks to my family, all the prayers, and the Great Mercy of Him. Praise God!"

I was crazy with joy, and began crying, and dancing all around the room!

"Hon, I have to go and tell the folks who've prayed for him for so long," I shouted and flew out the door. At each place I stopped to tell my friends the good news, we hugged and danced for joy.

At the last house, a charismatic friend was so happy for me that we went outside, danced and sang, lifted hands, and danced and sang some more!

Fig wondered where I was, as it was getting dark, and called around until he found me. The mercy that God had promised, no matter how alarming the judge's sentence, was the same great mercy Nate had recognized in his salvation.

Soon after I received Nate's card, we went out to the village for six weeks of translation work. At the end of that we returned to civilization, and I got in line at the Ukarumpa post office. While I waited, a friend tapped me on the shoulder and asked if I was going to the retreat in two days.

"What retreat?" I hadn't heard a thing about it. Even if I wanted to apply, the deadline had already passed. God, though, moved through friends. One urged the organizer to pry open a place for me, and another let me use her computer. Still another found me a seat for the five-hour ride to Madang, Papua New Guinea. I was off.

Women from Abilene Christian College were giving us missionaries a time of R & R at the lovely Jas Haben Resort, free! The women simply wanted to bless us, and they did it lavishly.

We studied Psalm 103. "Praise the LORD, my soul, and forget not all his benefits" (v. 2). After many years of waiting and trusting, God had answered our prayers and in his love had saved my son! I was overwhelmed with gratitude for his great mercy, and I wept with thanksgiving and praise for such a Father! I just could not get over his goodness.

Afternoons, we had such fun. We swam; we illustrated our favorite Bible verses; we sat by the water and talked as we ate fresh tropical delights—pineapple, papaya, bananas, and passion fruit. Evenings, we enjoyed a variety of activities, including crazy skits, and dancing, my favorite. There was one friend who had two left feet and was shy about joining in. I told her to hang on, let me lead, and I would help her shake a leg. I literally carried her like a rag doll around the dance floor! I laughed those evenings as much as I cried during the days.

That week there was such healing of my weary heart. I was with women who may have had different sorrows, but they all knew trouble, so I could release my tears without shame.

After seventeen years of holding on, it was heavenly to let go!

12

New Life

This was the beginning of new life for Nate, not the end to all his troubles. Just five months later, this was a portion of a letter from November 2009:

Dear Mom and Dad,

Got your letter yesterday, glad to hear things are coming together so that you can come back here. I'm going to Bible study 4 nights a week. It's run by the same people, but each night there's a different person leading. That's the main thing happening other than playing cards and trying to workout.

Mom, what you told me about Augustine fighting against himself is something I go through constantly. It is hard for me to put on the new man. I read about that in the New Testament; the same thing you spoke of what Augustine said about the reconstruction taking time gave me hope. 'Cause I still need some permanent reconstruction.

I should get my privileges back the end of this month. I can't wait to see you. Thanks for everything.

Love you,
Nate

We came home from PNG soon after that letter was written and visited Nate, maybe December 2009.

Dear Mom,

It was so good to see you after all this time. What a great surprise! I want to let you know some things by letter. Somehow when I'm face to face with any of y'all I can't really speak. I get real uncomfortable, anxious and defensive at times. And as soon as you leave I'm wondering what happened, and having all kinds of regrets about what I said or didn't say.

When I think about having a visit I try to set my mind that this next one will not be like that 'cause there's no reason for it.

I love you and you've done so much for me and are the only ones that really love me. But although seeing you again was one of the greatest things I still felt panicked and defensive. And even though I'm being worked on to become the new person in Christ Jesus I didn't even want to talk about it. I really don't like dealing in emotions either and I think that's a part (of it).

I just wanted to let you know that I love you. I know Jesus will work everything out. I think my nerves are a little shot so when I don't see you for a long time and then do, that's probably why in the past I didn't hardly eat sometimes on visits.

I asked Miriam for a book on sewing patterns (how to sew), and you said something about a book on just knots. That would be interesting too and cheap if you run across one. Love you so much, Mom, you look great! 😊

—Nate

March 2012

Man, I'm happy about your eye surgery [Fig's cataract surgery] being a success. I can't describe how it hit me when I learned that Uncle Joe had given in at the end. [Fig and I had heard from Christian friends that Fig's brother, Joe, had accepted Jesus a week before he died in the hospital.] So great is our God. I'll try to call tonight. I love and miss y'all something terrible. Thanks for being you.

—Nate

December 2012

Dear Mom,

Happy late, late Birthday! I'd been waiting to get a birthday card drawn but still haven't been able to make that happen. Strange coincidental issues have affected this plan. Still trying. I remember from time to time how you'd take time out to play badminton and tennis with me. It means more to me now than it did back then as an ignorant clown. Although I enjoyed it back then, I really wasn't able to appreciate it like I do now. The older I get, the more the puzzle comes together in things like "the big picture."

[He wrote about an anger management program, then about pets.]

Anyway, all my life I've liked dogs, and not cats but I like cats now. Any animal that appreciates the food I give it is a friend of mine. I want them happy too though, for the most part. And I really like exotic cats. I really want a bull terrier like Spuds MacKenzie [sic] the Budweiser dog that is white with a black eye. Do you know what I'm talking about, with a kinda long snout? They are short and strong and were bred to be fighting dogs, but everyone I've seen on TV is very happy and spunky. Same with all I've heard about them. Second choice is a Pit Bull. I read a large book on Pit Bulls and can't relay all the info. Certainly have to have a yard, certain location, certain dogs in the vicinity, certain serious training, etc. [went on about pit bulls for half a page]. Well, I'm about to let all spiders go. The flies are pretty much gone now that it's December. [Nate loved keeping a jar of spiders and feeding them, observing their habits.] I love you Mom. You are the very Best.

—Nate

In that same envelope there was another short letter. Nate had heard I was taking Benadryl for my allergy to bee stings, and he told me the best way to take the capsules:

Well, the capsules were something to talk about. I recently stopped taking all meds including Benadryl. God's made some great changes in me recently, and medication removal was one of them. I'm very thankful for that. I was just thinking about the pets we had. We had some really real neat animals. They use to have many seagulls here that would make seasonal stops throughout the year. Big flocks. But it's a charge if you feed them now so they are 95% gone. It's illegal to bring a biscuit or anything out of the café now anyway. Thanks for everything, Mom. I'll call around Christmas. It's Sunday night I'm done with these letters. Love you Mom, tell Dad I love him. —Nate

Early 2013

Mom,

It was so good to hear your voice that last time. Sometimes you just shine through. I can't really talk on the phone, but it's obvious I've been going through some things. But all that's over with now. I've been healed. Spiritually, mentally, and physically. I almost sold virtually all I had, spiritually, mentally and physically. But He stopped me and healed me. Why? He made it clear. "Too many prayers. Too many prayers." Praise God! And already he's using my past negative actions as positives in his perfect plan. Amazing.

Well, almost everyone is off restriction canteen, phone and visit. People can live again finally. Need to get this out.

Love you so much, Mom, and everyone.

—Nate

God was moved by the many prayers sent up for him from folks all over the world.

November 2016, almost four years after we received the early 2013 letter, Nate was released from prison. As we rejoiced with his freedom, we were only slightly aware of the many adjustments he would face. From the day of his release, we heard story after story of prison life. But as the weeks passed, Nate began to turn inside himself.

The talking ended. Fourteen years of incarceration rendered our son out-of-step with the fast-changing world, and Nate was feeling it. One day he and I were in town when he motioned at a young boy texting on his smartphone. "Mom, look at that kid. I feel like such a clown." At thirty-seven Nate felt he was enrolled in Life 101. His surroundings and schedules had all changed quickly and drastically. Instead of a six-by-eight-foot cell with a cell mate, he was with us and a ninety-eight-year-old grandmother, his Ganna. After losing his first job, he had regular landscaping work with three friends of mine. Nate didn't do drugs in our home, but was still self-prescribing, and that kept him from holding down daily work.

The four years of having him around were at once so good and *also* very nerve-racking. With all his spare time, I was relieved when he met a man who had a wood shop and furniture-refinishing business. This friendship gave Nate a place where he could do what he loved, work with his hands. I am grateful, too, that Nate had time with his Ganna. She loved him and was genuinely interested in his life, chatting whenever he gave her time. She remained a great Southern lady to her last day. Mom died at home, April 22, 2020. We began fixing the house to sell, preparing to move to Nebraska.

13

Heavenly Helper

Do you believe in angels?
We had one present himself at a horrific time in the summer of 2020. Nate was in jail on serious, but nonviolent, charges. It looked like he would be incarcerated for a good while.

I wrote in my journal, "was so fragile and was on the verge of tears after church." I was at an all-time low and felt utterly hopeless.

Nate was in such misery and had phoned us in his distress. The meds for his UTI had been confiscated at his arrest. His longtime, intermittent sciatica had returned, and he was dealing with that excruciating pain, as well as a toothache. Nate was the only one responsible for some of his predicaments. Aren't we glad, though, that God "does not treat us as our sins deserve or repay us according to our iniquities" (Psalm 103:10)?

Before Nate called us, he had been talking to a close friend out West who wanted to help, maybe

73

to the point of paying his bond, then hiring him to work off the debt. With this plan in the works, Fig and I were willing to contact the bondsman to handle Nate's release.

After answering Nate's call with this hopeful news of a release soon, he surprisingly attacked me with a barrage of complaints. "Now I've been made the fool, as I said you could get me out today! I've never brought bad friends to your house; I've been kind; no drugs there." On and on he ranted, ending with, "I'm just ready to chuck it all. Forget him, forget everything. I'm just going to kill myself!"

You might be wondering if he was just pressuring me to get his way. I can't say with certainty that you are wrong, but Nate had never talked about giving up. In all his troubled years I had never heard this extreme hopelessness, and I was so frightened. I felt as if Satan was smothering him with his darkness, whispering in his ear to choose this deadly solution to his distress.

What do you do when your child is in grave danger of destroying himself and you can do absolutely nothing to stop him?

I ran and told my husband the rash course Nate was considering. Fig held me and prayed while I wept. Next, I called a dear friend, who prayed with me against Satan's lies. God did protect Nate. The next morning the bondsman came, and he was released.

The day before Nate was to fly out West, he brought a known prostitute, who was very pregnant, home to help him go through the storage shed out back. I knew of this pretty young woman, having helped street people before. I also was fairly sure that my son would not be so bold as to bring home someone he was involved with.

I welcomed her. They worked from morning to night, first helping a friend move, then packing Nate for his early-morning trip. After they finished, I fixed supper for her.

Nate said he'd take the woman home and be back later. By then it was nine p.m., rainy, and the dirt roads muddy. I was afraid he'd miss his flight if he stayed out too late. It was a nonrefundable ticket, and his friend was waiting at the other end.

Although more than a bit anxious, I was able to sleep, and early that next morning Nate was home when it was time to leave. Thinking back over the years, and the many occasions when he'd said he would meet me somewhere, he had always shown up. It is remarkable, as he has never owned a watch and has often been without a phone.

Oh yes, about the angel. Nate had been incarcerated for seventeen years, and hadn't flown since the early nineties. Still, he wasn't ready to take any pointers from us. He had one connection to make, in a huge airport, with only an hour. I was thinking, *How in the world will he make his connecting flight!* He needed help from above.

As we walked from the ticket counter, he said he needed a smoke, and reached in his pocket.

"Whoa! Not here," I warned, and pushed him toward the exit.

"Where can you smoke?" I asked a woman standing nearby. She smiled, pointing overhead to the sign that read Smoking Area. We saw a young man across the way lighting up, so Nate hugged me good-bye and said he'd buy a smoke off this guy.

As I walked to the car, I looked back and saw the two had finished their cigarettes and were talking as they entered the terminal. That was the helper we needed, Nate's angel, a smoking one at that!

He made it to his destination and worked for nearly half a year in a lovely setting. I will never get over this marvelous show of God's kindness and mercy.

14

A Dog and Change

Fig and I left North Carolina to move to Nebraska at Christmastime in 2020. Nate, in South Carolina, was soon homeless, living in a shelter in the woods. Two years later, he had this story to tell:

Mom, I found this great dog, named her Lunchbox. She is the best dog ever, smart, and you know how other dogs look away, she always looks right into my eyes. She won't attack other dogs, and stays right near me when I tell her to. The other day she and I were sitting on the side of the road and a car stopped to give me a couple of bottles of water. Mom, people are always giving me things for my dog, like leashes, dog collars, food and the like. It was a warm day, and these folks wanted to help. Just then a police car pulled up and arrested me for soliciting on a public road!

Nate was in jail again, and this time someone other than he was affected—his beloved dog.

I began trying to locate Lunchbox and see if the animal shelter folks might keep her until Nate was released. I was in the Midwest, and Nate and his dog were far away. I was on the phone several times a day, but those I talked to refused to tell me where the dog was. I didn't look forward to evenings when Nate called for news about her and there was none.

He thought I should try harder, but his lost dog wasn't all he was dealing with. This correctional facility gave such small meals to the inmates that Nate was walking four hours a day simply to take his mind off how hungry he was. Sometimes, as he walked, he imagined how he might prepare Lunchbox's food for his own meal, if only he'd had some. Not only did the jail feed them a scanty supper; it was at 3:30, and this meal had to last until breakfast the next day!

I was so concerned about Nate's dog, his hunger, his drug use, and how God was going to meet all these desperate needs. I had learned through many years of knowing God that he had Nate in mind when Jesus died. So I knew he had a vested interest in this sheep of his.

The Good Shepherd story—found in John 10:1–18—has encouraged me many times when my son was suffering and there was little I could do. In verses 11–13, Jesus says that he is not like the hired man. When the wolf comes to attack the sheep, the hired man runs away because it's above his pay grade to risk his life. In contrast, the Good Shepherd loves his sheep and will do whatever it takes to protect them.

Would this same Jesus, who died for his sheep, not take care of Nate, his lamb, who was hungry? Nate was physically hungry and could think of little else, but in his deepest soul he was also starved for life and peace.

I cried out to God to meet him there in that jail, to speak to him through the Bible he was reading again, and move him along to the next step in God's rescue plan for him.

I'm reading now from my journal entry, October 2022. My daily reading was Psalm 12, focusing on verse 5, "Because of the oppression of the weak and the groaning of the needy, I will now arise, says the Lord. "I will place him in the safety for which he longs." (ESV) I praised God that morning for hearing Nate's groans, and that God would arise at just the right time and put him in the safe place he longed for. I knew my Father had heard my prayers, so I was able to go on with life, and not worry about my boy. His postcard came a few days later.

October 22, 2022

Dear Mom,

Thank you so much for all you've done especially with the dog. I've decided not to sweat Lunchbox anymore. Just to let God handle this, since he already knows. I hate I don't show it, but I love you Mom. Tell my relatives hello with love, and Dad too.
—Nate

It was just days after the postcard arrived that Nate called and said he was going to drug rehab for the first time! We had urged him to go when he was in Opportunity School, but he hadn't been ready then, and until he was, we'd just "waste our money." I'd appreciated his honesty. Many parents have spent thousands on rehab, many of those to no avail. But Nate was signing himself in.

Oh, I was beyond elated! I had waited twenty-five years for this. God alone had heard our pleas and was placing my son in that "safe place"—and in his own time.

I knew nothing about the rehab program Nate had chosen; I just hoped it was good. He had been in jail now a handful of months, but he hadn't even met his public defender. Until Nate's case was decided, he wasn't going anywhere.

He asked me to call his PD to find out when his name might come up. I had hardly introduced myself when the PD told me the case would be heard that next day. (One does wonder if hearing from a concerned person on the outside gets the ball rolling on the inside.)

Since he seemed such a nice man, I asked if he knew anything about the rehab program Nate had named. For a minute it was as if the phone had gone dead. Then in a broken voice he answered, "Ma'am, they saved my boy's life."

I could have cried right then and there. Instead, I thanked the man and hung up. Then I cried tears of gratitude. *Thank you, dear Father, for this huge step in Nate's life. You alone have done this—and with a program Nate's PD gave a firsthand thumbs-up to.* The pieces were falling into place, and I knew it was God.

Nate got out of jail on December 2, 2022, but without a car, with no place to stay, and with three whole days before he would actually sign in to rehab. Anything could happen in seventy-two hours. But there was a person in place who had stepped up a year earlier. Telly was part of a group of men who prayed but didn't just sit around praying. They also had food fit for men, and fun, like blowing up 150 Halloween pumpkins with Tannerite.

This man had gone early to the meeting one night when Fig called the host to see if anyone there would be willing to make the fifty-mile trip to deliver a message to Nate. He happily volunteered. Later, when I heard it from Telly, he added, "It was so unlike me to be there a half hour early."

From then on, Telly was the helping hand I needed to reach out to Nate. This man knew what it was like to need a leg up, and it was he who drove my son to rehab.

God always answers prayer, moms. It's not on our time, but it's always on time. We need to trust God, and trust him again.

15

I Know a Friend

With Nate it was just par for the course.

One early morning in October 2023, we bought our fixed tickets to visit friends in the Carolinas and to see Nate.

Hours later, I heard an all-too-familiar greeting: "This is a call from an inmate at the county detention center."

My heart sank. Nate was in jail again, and I might not get to see my boy at all!

Here is what had happened. Several months before, Nate was walking past a local towing business on his way to his place in the woods. An employee, whom Nate knew, stopped to tell him that a fob had been stolen and that he himself would have to cough up the money if he couldn't locate it.

Nate told him he'd see what he could learn at the camp. In a little while he returned the fob to a happy employee, no questions asked.

Now, three months later, Nate had been arrested. When he called us, he was so miffed at the injustice done by this employee on whom he had had pity. The police were holding him until he told them who had stolen it.

Fear was knocking at my door. Like any loving mother who hasn't seen her son in three years, I just wanted to be near him. As I sat cross-legged on my bed considering this new wrinkle, I was convinced God had led us to buy the tickets. So, I wondered, had he changed his plans? Was he toying with me, or had he somehow forgotten our friendship?

When in doubt, check his Word. "But I have called you friends, for all that I have heard from my Father I have made known to you" (John 15:15 ESV). Like a friend, God leads us. This does not mean that he answers us right when we ask. If he waits, he does it for our good.

Left to myself, I could have become so anxious over these new obstacles. A passage that has regularly reined me in is, "Do not be anxious about anything, but in every situation, by prayer and petition, with thanksgiving, present your requests to God. And the peace of God which transcends all understanding, will guard your hearts and your minds in Christ Jesus" (Philippians 4:6–7). God tells me to stop being anxious that Nate is in jail.

How can that be? It's because we have a God who can, and will, do the very best for us. That's what we are trying to do for our kids, but we make mistakes. He doesn't. I began praying right then for him to take over and make this time away exactly what he wanted—for us and for Nate.

During these days with our friends, Nate kept in touch with us from jail. There were some problems that God was going to have to solve, if we were to see him.

First, Nate had seen the judge sign the paper setting the bond at four thousand dollars. But when we called the bondsman, he said the authorities wanted twenty thousand. Bail is one tenth of the bond. We had already agreed with Nate to pay no more than six hundred dollars. He was sure that someone was jacking up the price to keep him locked up and pressure him to rat on his acquaintances.

Who would pay the balance of the bail? Nate had given us the name of a woman who could help. On the way to the bondsman, we picked her up. Although she had never met Nate, she had agreed to sign for the bail. In the homeless community Deb was a willing associate.

This was Saturday, our last day in the Carolinas. The bondsman was working only that morning. The three of us sat in Jamaine's office while he checked

Deb's record. It was clear right away that she was a regular in the system. She even had an outstanding bill for another inmate's bail. Oops! Chances were slim that he would accept her promise to pay.

Next, the bondsman scrolled through Nate's record, noting only that Nate's bond was coming up as four thousand in one place, twenty thousand in another. Earlier that morning, Jamaine's coworker had said of the discrepancy, "Someone has a fat finger." No matter who had done it, Jamaine was now certain that the bond was twenty thousand.

Finally, he voiced the inevitable: "No, your six hundred dollars is too little to cover a twenty-thousand bond."

I could easily have burst into tears over his refusal. Airplane tickets had cost us a tidy sum; we had come a long way, now with no hope of seeing our dear son. Surprisingly, I wasn't sad. There were no tears, for I knew it was not over.

I clearly remember thinking, *This man is convinced that he is in control of this case. He's mistaken. God himself will determine what happens today.* I had such peace and walked out of the office knowing Jamaine's word was not the last.

Deb was texting the whole time, trying to console us by saying, "I know people." She directed us to another office, where the parking lot was empty.

Fig pulled the car up in the shade of a tree, and we waited.

I was tempted to say, *I know someone too, Deb. He is a "friend who sticks closer than a brother," and he is at work.*

As we sat wondering what to do next, I recalled that Nate had recently said, "Mom, if you pay the six hundred dollars, I'll pay the rest." As Fig and I talked, we decided that Nate could handle it. He had been working regularly for the couple we were staying with that night. So we returned to the bondsman's office to pay bail and sign papers for the balance.

We had only to wait for Nate to be released. What had seemed impossible God had done. I would get to see my son that day! Then came the tears, but these were of pure joy.

As we walked around the parking lot, I searched each black police van, straining to glimpse Nate's silhouette through the tinted glass. It was two long hours. I have learned that few city or state workers are in a hurry when it comes to inmates. I've also learned that God's care for his people goes beyond what we can imagine.

Fig had strolled some distance away when our bondsman exited the county jail, holding something. He came directly to me, stating without explanation,

"Looks like the bond was four thousand dollars, so I owe you two hundred."

Nate was right. I could not suppress a smile or keep my hand from patting Jamaine's shoulder with thanks. God was present, and he, not a man, was in charge. When unsure of what to do, we had waited for his instructions, and he had led. We must be on speaking terms, telling God our needs, and be serious about listening to him. Extended waits are hard, but when it's time to take the next step, he does let us know. After all, he is our friend.

16

What Is God up To?

On that November 2023 trip to the Carolinas, one thing that struck me, after spending four hours with Nate, is that I do not know, I cannot know, what God is doing in his life.

Our hosts were still at their jobs, so we three sat in their back yard. Fig and I enjoyed the swing in the lovely seventy-degree weather, while Nate, fresh out of jail, took stock of his gear. Living in the woods, he has to carry most of his possessions. We had two uninterrupted hours, just mom, dad, and son, while he sorted through his two backpacks—the closets, shelves, and drawers of my homeless one.

After some time passed, I needed to find a bathroom, and the rental car needed gas, so Nate drove me around the corner to a station.

When I came out through the swinging door, Nate was there talking to an old homeless man who was hunched over, sitting on the curb.

He introduced his friend. "Mom, this is Chewy."

I took his dry, gnarled hand and greeted him.

Then Nate surprised me with, "Mom, would you pray for Chewy? He's had a hard week; so many bad things have come up."

I took his hand again, and while Nate laid his on the man's shoulders, I prayed.

When I looked up, I saw that an older woman had joined us. She wore a stocking-cap and was holding what looked like a bedroll. I caught only the last part of their muted exchange as Nate told the woman, "He's in the hospital." It sounded as if he was urging her to go see the man.

After visiting our forty-four-year-old in his digs, my best guesses about what exactly is going on in his life have changed.

Over many years, Nate has repeatedly said, "Mom, you assume so much when you really don't know." That's what moms do, if we're not kept informed. What I saw happen that afternoon wasn't what I envisioned Nate doing. He was not ingenuous, so I knew his interactions with the others was typical of him. My son knows I believe in prayer, so it was natural for him to ask me to pray for his friend.

As he drove, he informed me, "Mom, Chewy is a devil worshiper, and I mean, really. The woman, Alma, relays prophecies that birds tell her about me." He wanted me to know how needy his community is.

As to God's plans for Nate, at this point I have many more questions than answers. My son, several years earlier, had called and said, "Mom, I've been changed, and you don't know how much!"

But I had no idea what that change might involve. I hadn't seen him for a long time. This glimpse into his world reminds me of the quote from Elisabeth Elliot, propped on my windowsill, that reads, "God is God. Because He is God, He is worthy of my trust and obedience. I will find rest nowhere but in His holy will, *a will that is unspeakably beyond my largest notion of what He is up to*" (emphasis mine).

What I saw of Nate's life led me to pray differently for him. We may think, *Oh, God's not doing anything. My boy is in jail again, or back with his girlfriend, or whatever undesirable situation one's wanderer is in.* Even in the Bible, God has often used an awful place, like prison, for good. What if Joseph had not been jailed because of the lonely wife's false accusation? He would not have been in a position to save the Israelites. If Daniel had not been confined to a lion's den, King Darius would not have seen the miracle of closing the lions' mouths and would not have decreed that all in his kingdom must worship the God of Daniel.

Nate, in his own setting, demonstrated the change he'd told me about.

He has always cared about people. Seven years before, when we were taking care of Fig's mom in her home and Nate was just out of prison, he regularly used his truck to help move people evicted from their homes. He explained that where he presently lives his homeless community is not near the soup kitchens one hears about. Yes, there are businesses that regularly discard edible food and other items in dumpsters nearby. If he times it right, he can get there before folks drive up and take everything good, probably to sell. Whatever he gets, he shares with others. His distributing and his reaching out, like at the gas station, was a snapshot of how God is using my son. It is truly "beyond my largest notion of what He is up to."

17

Life Today

Here is a conversation I had with Nate on June 24, 2024. I learned something about his living conditions and saw how God has been providing for him and for others through him.

"How's your life going?"

"I'm just going from A to B, I guess."

"Victoria [my friend who loves Nate] talks you up. She was saying that the church makes people think they have to be perfect."

"Yeah."

"It's not what Jesus did. And the religious people hated him."

"Right."

"Victoria hopes you can be used for people on the street. Are you comfortable where you live? Are there a lot of violent people?"

"No, not on the surface. There's always different levels."

"Do you feel safe?"

(pause)

"Yeah, I mean, yeah. Why do you ask that?"

"Is it quiet, or noisy? Do people go to sleep at night?"

"I'm in the woods. Yeah, it's pretty nice."

"Do you have space between you and the next guy?"

"I don't think there's anybody staying in these woods I'm in. Things can change any moment, but I don't think there's anybody. These are crazy woods; they've got locust trees. I don't know which kind, but if you get hit with the thorns, it gets infected. Kinda when I first came out here, about six months ago, after a month, a cop came out here and, after making an arrest of someone else, said the owners don't mind if people stay here, just don't clear the land or leave trash or garbage. But there's black locust, I think he said, and if you get struck by a thorn, you'll have to go to the hospital; it'll get infected. And that kinda answered a question I'd had. I was getting sores, and I didn't know what they were. It was that. I didn't know what was going on. Thorns can come up later, sometimes in different areas. I think that's another reason people don't go back here."

"They don't bother you now; you're able to keep away from them?"

"I've been stuck a bunch of times; it's not infecting me anymore; maybe getting resistant. At first it was like ulcers; that's what was happening. They say the whole tree is toxic. May be honey [locust], green [locust]? I don't know. There's at least three kinds."

"What can I do to help you?"

"A storage unit would be nice. You can get it for twenty dollars a month for the first month, then it goes up. There's this one guy, I don't know where he's at. Something like that would help. You can store your stuff, safely, and I don't have to tote it everywhere, which I'm doing now."

"How have you been doing with J and K [friends Nate works for]? Still working for them?"

"I have not been over there for two weeks." (pause) "I don't know; I feel they expected more, you know what I mean, which I totally understand."

"You just don't want a regular job? What seems to be the problem?"

"I can't get over there every day. Like I told them from the gate, don't expect me to be there every day. When I leave, by morning I might be a whole day's walk away, and then by nighttime I might be asleep, I might sleep through the next day or something and can't make it back, you know, so the schedule's messed up. There's been a lot of times when they've wanted me to help them do something, and I've been willing to do it, you know. You get out there, and you walk and you walk. I carry a pack; I just now got a wagon, just found it about two hours ago, with a bunch of stuff all strewn out. I just threw all the stuff away and kept the wagon. I think I know whose it was, but they didn't want it. Usually, I'm just carrying my stuff, right? I've got so much. I've been using a Target shopping cart for maybe a week. I can carry a lot more stuff than just walking with it, carrying it. Backpacks are tearing apart, all of them. But it's just I had so much weight for so long it's tearing apart. I've been using that buggy. And now, I've got this wagon. Yeah, so what I'm saying, after doing all that, when I get where I'm going, when I go to sleep, ain't no telling when I'm goin' to wake up. So it doesn't fit. I've been putting it off, even though I can help them. Man, I hate going through this, you know what I mean."

"I want to help you, not put a burden on you. Do you need a backpack? Tell us what you need, and we'll get it for you."

"I've got shopping carts. I'm good, really. I'm not even getting into that now. These mosquitoes are biting me, Mom. I need to get somewhere before it's too late."

"I'm sending you this Walmart card. Okay to send it to J and K's?"

"Thanks, Mom."

"Keep in touch with us; we love you."

"Love you too; sorry I haven't called in so long. You can call me anytime, whenever. If I don't answer, it doesn't mean . . . it's not like you're bothering me or nothin'. Keep calling. If I can, I'll answer it. You ain't never aggravatin' me."

(Nate has always been a fine language learner. You can tell who he'd been hanging out with.)

"We love you so much."

"I love you too. Dad too."

Finding out where he lives, and that the landowners are alright with his being there, was such a comfort to me. During Nate's years in prison, and his past three years on his own, my boy has been regular in contacting me. "Regular" is a bit longer between calls than I'd like, but time and again, just when the wait begins to trouble me, he calls.

The following is another conversation, two months later, when I learned even more about Nate's living situation and had offered him a Walmart card, mainly for food.

"I hate to have asked you."

"Son, you didn't ask me; I asked you. I know what food costs; I go to the store."

"It's crazy."

"It *is* crazy."

"You can't get a meal for five dollars almost. And like, at Taco Bell, I've had three dollars and asked them to give me as much of anything as they could, right? And it's nighttime, so they say, first, you can't get in the door, right, so you gotta go through the drive-through. No, you've got to be in a car. Are you serious? They wouldn't serve me. So I just stood where the speakers are, where people pull in, and said, 'Hey, man, can you just get me as many tacos as you can for three bucks?' You know, I figured they'd call the police because I was interfering, but luckily the first person was like, 'Yeah, I got you,' and just didn't even make me pay. He got me three tacos."

"Wonderful, wonderful."

"It just depends, you know what I'm saying, who it is. It goes for everything."

"Have you been healthy?"

"I'm just tired, you know. I'm just tired."

"Do you sleep?"

"Yeah. It's just hard to get food sometimes. There's no soup kitchens or nothing. If it's not in the dumpster or I don't come here [to J and K's], then it's like, you just gotta kinda find, you know . . . it ain't no three meals a day. It just doesn't work like that. It is what it is, though. Ain't a thing you can do about it. Sometimes they'll do an inventory, one store or another, and they'll throw away a bunch of stuff. Like this store had salmonella or something, so they had to throw a bunch of stuff away, three dumpsters full, all at once; you get what you can, but it don't last long, cause it's possibly salmonella, so you don't want to keep it long. Then it's dry again, you know; then there's nothing for a while, and then another dumpster might have it, you never know. But it's not consistent. So, it's kind of like the hyena, I guess; when you get a meal, you just gorge."

"You know, I so wish you could be involved in a church, somebody that'll care for you."

"Huh?"

"They're open to all sorts of folks."

"Yeah."

"If you find the right one, they'll take you in."

"Yeah. Well, let me get her phone back. I've got to walk. I got to go to a couple of places."

"Son, you know your dad and I think you're at the top of the heap."

"Love you all."

The more I hear about how Nate gets his food, the more urgent his deliverance from all drugs becomes. The Enemy loves to accuse and whisper, *You've missed your chance to help him. It's your fault, Susan, that he's not further along in his Christian walk.*

I know that's a lie. God doesn't need me to do his work. I'm reminded again that this is God's battle. I do have questions like, *Where does giving that "cup of cold water" fit in? If I help him with food, how much do I give to him and not delay God's plan?* Hmm, only God knows, and he will guide me, for "the LORD has compassion on those who fear him . . . he remembers that we are dust" (Psalm 103:13–14).

On some days, you moms will have changing concerns and questions as you hear from your wanderer, or not hear at all. Remember, God is your friend, if you've let him befriend you. Since he's never put off, you can talk plainly to him, even when you're full of questions and doubts.

PART TWO

THOUGHTS FROM
THE STORY

18

Credible Witness

God made us to be part of a group, the Church, Christ's body. We were never meant to stand alone. When you're a mom of a struggling child, you need other moms who have had similar heartaches, awful disappointments, defeats, and some victories. We need them now more than ever.

Let me tell you about a time when God brought such a person into my life. She helped me tremendously in a struggle I was having, not with my son, but with my husband.

After Fig and I married on September 11, 1971, we had three rocky years.

My husband was a very black and white sort. No grays, please. We were both in Bible school at Columbia Graduate School of Bible and Missions (now Columbia International University). That may suggest that we had it pretty much together. Wrong.

Fig was examining the truths of God's Word for the first time. His family had gone to a liberal church that did not teach that Scripture has no error and that the Word alone teaches what God wants us to believe and do. The Lord's desire was that, through the truth of the Bible, Fig would find out how much God loved him and experience the deep, real, and permanent good he wanted to do in and through him.

But the Enemy, the devil and deceiver of all men, had other plans. Fig, in his cubicle each day after classes, sat alone with his Bible, and the battle began. He studied the Scriptures and sound theology of the character of God, knowing him, obeying him, even loving him, and agreed in his heart.

The devil whispered, *There's no way you can or will do this. You are complicit in your weakness, and you know it.* Back and forth the battle in Fig's mind raged. He came home each day exhausted, frustrated, and often explosive.

As his wife, the shrapnel whizzed in my direction. One night at bedtime, Fig turned to me and growled, "I'm going straight to hell, and don't you say I'm not!"

I can remember my eyes being as big as saucers, and I knew I'd not open my mouth to refute him.

God was very gracious to me. I knew about prayer. I believed God would save Fig from the sense of being condemned, and hopeless to change, which Satan was causing in him.

Along with this spiritual confidence, God sent a living being to help me. One day in chapel I heard a middle-aged Christian leader say that she and her husband had had struggles in their early years. She was the first woman I'd heard confess distress like mine. I had to talk with her!

Funny, but I'd expected this older woman to listen to how I had suffered with Fig's troubles, put her loving arms around me, and tell me how brave I'd been to persevere.

Was I ever mistaken! Mrs. B asked me what I had done to help my husband in this time of awful turmoil under Satan's harassment. She was curious about my response to his pain, not his response to mine. She urged me to be a good listener, and to keep praying earnestly for him.

I felt like a ten-year-old when she admonished me to be done with this "poor me" attitude and, at twenty-five, to grow up. Finally, she challenged me to be Fig's strong support, instead of needing his. All this was wise counsel. I listened because I knew she cared for me and that she had learned these truths firsthand.

So, you moms who've seen God come through in your distress, act on that nudge to tell your story. To another hurting mom, you are a credible witness, one who has believed God, and can offer firsthand hope.

19

Am I to Blame?

For those of you who have tried everything—counseling, special classes, shadowing your adolescent in school, tutors, laying on of hands by the elders, more discipline, less discipline, talking, not talking, and, oh yes, praying, fasting, and it just hasn't worked, don't lose heart. You trusted God to guide you in those helpful activities for your child. Continue to trust that he will use them for good. Maybe you don't see changes yet. But seeds have been planted in their hearts and minds. It takes time for the shoots to appear.

By his steadfast love and mercy God helps us to believe he's working in our rebel, and we wait. Elisabeth Elliot reminds us that the bird on her eggs waits patiently. She's programmed. We mothers, on the other hand, have choices. I tend to think that having to wait must be related to a shortcoming of *mine*. There is something *I* haven't done. *I* must be holding up his blessing. *I* have missed hearing God's voice. The tempter focuses our attention on the wait, makes us think it is unnecessary, and causes us to feel guilty for it. Don't fall into his trap. Our waiting doesn't mean he's late. God has a plan for our wanderers. The hows and whens of the process are wholly in his hands.

As you're waiting, ask God for verses on his attributes that you can think about. Or ask him for one of his promises that you can claim as his assurance to you (2 Peter 1:3–4). You are his daughter, and he delights to give what you desire. "You may ask me for anything in my name, and I will do it" (John 14:14). "In his name" means we can ask, appealing to his authority and with the privilege we have as his royal daughter, one who wants her Father's name to be held high.

I was considering how quickly Nate's life is passing when a question came to mind. Exactly how much would I have to fast for God to move in a big way on his behalf, delivering him from drugs, healing him at the root of all his cravings? How many ordinary but earnest prayers does it take to move God to work more quickly than he is?

In that same moment, God spoke, "*Susan, what are you thinking? Are you trying to convince me to sympathize with you by fasting, forcing me to act by your long, serious prayers?*"

No, Lord, that is not it. It reminds me of Sarai taking things into her own hands and urging Abram to produce an heir by her maid. Ishmael was, and still is trouble to Israel. I certainly do not want the negative consequences of going ahead of you. Schemes of fasting to add points to a score card or begging you more zealously to coax you into acting now*—neither is remembering and being true to who you are, or the way you act.*

20

Hang On

When I think of what it means to hang on to a truth, or to Jesus himself, I remember a close call I had as a little girl.

I loved the water and was not afraid of much. My mom and dad, my three brothers, ages six, two, and six months, and I, age four, were at a summer camp. We were headed to the lake, and I ran ahead of the family to be first to the dock.

But instead of waiting, I jumped right into the deep! I remember looking up from the dark and seeing a hand reach down through the light above. I stretched my hand upward, touched his fingers, and Dad pulled me out.

In my times of great sorrow, I would have been swallowed by dark waters, had my heavenly father not reached out to me. He tells us, "In this world you will have trouble" (John 16:33). These troubles are of all stripes: those caused by someone else, many of our own making, like young Susan recklessly plunging in, or others of natural causes. Whatever the trouble that has buried us, we need a Savior.

"But take heart I have overcome the world," he assures us (John 16:33). It never escapes him when we, his children, are hurting and in a hopeless mess. He knows when we cry out to him or when we're drowning and can't utter a sound (Luke 19:10). God will reach down, take hold, and deliver us out of the waters, just like my dad did with me.

21

It Was Necessary

I was studying the book of Luke in the summer of 2023, and reached the last chapter, one of my favorites.

Two disciples are walking to the town of Emmaus. As they go on, Jesus joins them, but the two don't recognize him. The friends are recounting the earth-shaking events they had just witnessed in Jerusalem, but the third man seems unaware of it all.

The pair goes on to say how Jesus, their master and friend, was betrayed by the religious leaders. With a pained expression one explained, "Jesus is dead, and we had hoped he was the Messiah" (author's paraphrase). At this point Jesus has heard enough and breaks in.

"O foolish ones, and slow of heart to believe all that the prophets have spoken! Was it not necessary that the Christ should suffer these things and enter into his glory?" (Luke 24:25–26 ESV).

As I read the words, "Was it not necessary?" his question spoke to me about suffering and its usefulness.

The Spirit offered, *"Susan, just as it was necessary for Jesus to suffer and bear the burden of sin before experiencing the glory of resurrection day, it is necessary that you bear the pain of watching your son suffer hardship from the consequences of his bad decisions. Like Jesus, if you yourself don't suffer, and wrestle with the anguish of a broken heart, how can you share in his suffering? The glory of knowing him is the result of depending on him. It is also necessary that Nate despair of himself so that I can do what I have intended all along, to bring glory to the Father's name through Nate's deliverance."*

God's acts of rescue always take longer than we want. Don't be in such a hurry, moms, to have the hard times go away. It hurts like crazy to watch our kids bear the results of their sins. But the suffering, it's necessary before God brings glory.

22

A Tough Season

I'm discouraged today. When God says, "*Stand firm*," I'm asking, *How long, O Lord? My feet burn from standing in one place; my legs get weak and heavy in this wait of trust and obey. I do find relief on my knees calling out to you for help. And some days I'm able to be still and know that you are God. Other days, I need your help to keep looking to you, and not at Nate, where he seems to be, and what he might be up to. It's the waiting that hurts—not a month or a year but years, Lord, many years.*

I miss my son, my dear, dear son. I miss his voice. I miss hugs or just putting my hand on his shoulder. I miss hearing his take on issues of the day. True, I do not miss the pounding demands, his insistent arguments, his pattern of seeing only his side, pressuring me to agree with him until I'm ready to yell, "Okay, enough; whatever, son!"

Open my eyes, Lord, and make me see your goodness as I wait for his deliverance. And when doubts assail, be my strength and my song (Psalm 118:14). Remind me of your promise that your words, which Nate has been taught through the years, will not return empty, will not be void of substance, but will do the work you sent them to do (Isaiah 55:11). You comfort me with, "Susan, think back and see my faithfulness; look closely and remember my goodness to you and to him. I'm true to my word. Don't be discouraged, my daughter."

These words from Amy Carmichael have given me hope while I wait:

Doubt not, He will not wait too long,

Fear not, He will not come too late.[1]

---

[1] Amy Carmichael, quoted in L. B. Cowman, *Streams in the Desert*, ed. James Riemann (Zondervan, 2016), 278.

23

Daily Prayers

I hadn't been married long before an older woman I was with in a small prayer group taught me the ACTS of prayer. I needed an orderly way to approach God in my morning devotion time, and this was it.

Adoration, the "A" in the mnemonic, is the proper way to approach the God of heaven, but I need concrete attributes to think on as I worship. I begin each morning by reading a psalm. To keep to a schedule, I begin with Psalm 1 on the first day of one month. The next month, I am at Psalm 31, etc. If I spend two days on one psalm, so be it. I spend time with the psalmist meditating on those features of God's being and praising him for several of them.

Confession is the "C." This can be a bit harder for me, and sometimes I forget to do it. But each day I do ask the Holy Spirit to take the portion of the Word I'm reading and use it to change me. I want to be more like Jesus.

"T" is for thanksgiving. I usually have much to thank him for, but on hard days I may draw a blank. So I thank Jesus for dying to pay for my sins. Pondering his great act of mercy produces even more praise and gratefulness.

"S" is the first thing we think about with the word *prayer*, but it's last in order. This is supplication, when I ask God for what I need or want for myself and others. As the psalmist puts it, "To the Lord I cry aloud, and he answers me from his holy hill." (Psalm 3:4 ESV), and Psalm 65:2 says, "O you who hear prayer, to you all men will come." He hears what I'm asking him. Hallelujah!

God moved men by his Holy Spirit to write the thirty-nine books of the Old Testament and the twenty-seven of the New Testament. They tell of God and his design to rescue people by the death of his only Son, Jesus, so we can be made righteous. Then we are brought back into a right relationship with our Creator. When we pray, we join with him in what he is doing to bring this wandering child to salvation, or to a fuller commitment to his Lord. Both salvation and growth in Christ—sanctification—take prayer and time.

24

Homeless, Not Aimless

Prison changed Nate's life. He had been incarcerated for fourteen years in one stretch. I was not prepared to understand the effects so long a time had on our son's life.

There are people, though, who do understand. Nate met one of these recently, on a park bench. This man had been in prison and knows what my son is up against: the fears, uncertainties, and lack of routine that he lives with on the outside. This fellow gave him his number and said he will help, if Nate ever wants it. This incidental meeting I recognize as an "I'm still here" from my Father.

When I consider the years of waiting, in terms of eternity, it isn't so bad that Nate's life has had many twists and turns, ups and downs. Through the years he has spontaneously testified to changes that God has made in him. He has had unusual experiences, for sure, yet God's mercy is plain to see even in these.

So what am I so impatient about? It's my desire to help God get the job done, and now. Maybe I could step in and finally, toward the end of my life, push Nate a bit, say the magic words, or add to what's been done and finish this. God might allow it. But, shoot, I would be a fool to mess with his plan. His ways are so much higher than my puny ways, and his thoughts so much greater and, yes, better (Isaiah 55:9).

Forgive me, Father. I'm certain that if I leave you to act in your time and in your way, in the end I will bow and worship you for doing all things well.

25

Will He Fit?

It looked like our son just did not fit in, anywhere. I cannot know the whole story, that special spot in history, the place in the puzzle created with only Nate in mind. I do not mean pounding a square peg into a round hole. Instead his Creator is steadily cutting on him here and filing away a bit there.

I wish I could peep at the picture on the box, but that's not mine to see. The master puzzle-maker uses each event, many which do not seem ideal at the time, to create the perfect piece in the end. I cannot understand how a certain event in his life, or a particular characteristic, can possibly make him suitable.

Beware! The devil will move you to throw up your hands and think, *God made an awful blunder here; there's simply no place for his kind.*

Don't believe it. True, the Creator is not finished with him yet, but one day this man will be complete, and everything will drop into place.

26

Leaving Fantasy Land

Disney's music, the line that says, "A dream is a wish your heart makes when you're fast asleep," and Tinkerbell painting the sky with her pixie dust wand used to thrill my little girl heart. My dreams would surely come true.

I had such a good childhood, a mom and dad who loved Jesus, one another, and us. Dad was the authoritative one, and being a lieutenant colonel in the U.S. Marine Corps, he knew how to keep his troops in order. We all wanted to please him. Mom, on the other hand, was more fun-loving, and our obedience usually came only after she used her louder "I mean it" voice.

Dreaming began early for me: a husband and children, four kids like Mom, was at the top of my list. I loved being part of a big family. My three brothers and I spent almost endless days playing ball, cowboys and Indians, and frolicking at the beach.

Peter Pan realized that "the crocodile of time is always chasing us." It chased me. I grew up and married.

My American dream was not something I thought of "when I was fast asleep." Like all culture, it was caught—from family, from friends at school, from the neighborhood. Rear your children to love God and to play sports of some sort. (Yes, in the South, sports and God were both revered.) Boys and girls take piano lessons, learn to read music, and be part of band and chorus. Children are encouraged to do well in school without much help, to respect adults, and to obey them, whether or not they are their parents. When old enough, you earn money—girls babysit and later waitress. Boys mow lawns, have a paper route, or both. A teen works summers at least. I felt the dream was from God, a sort of holy edict that I would carry out for my family.

Then came our son, who did not conform to my ideals.

Little by little I saw my dreams fade. I prayed and begged God for answers to know how to deal with him. Nate had a very sensitive spirit and had believed in Jesus at a young age. But he lived life on the edge. He was forthright and didn't mind ruffling feathers. This was a boy who was not going to follow the normal path. Whether from nature or nurture, it is a fact that he had other genes, different birth parents, and an uncommon purpose for his life.

With few dreams left, I was empty, thrown on the Lord. I cried to him. He answered me and urged me to turn my attention from my boy and his many problems to God himself. The more he spoke, the more I realized that my dreams for Nate were faulty, broken, and petty. They had to be. They were mine, not God's.

Lord, then show me your dreams, and I'll pray for those to be brought to pass.

"No, Susan. My plans are far too great for you to know."

"Oh, the depth of the riches of the wisdom and knowledge of God! How unsearchable his judgments, and his paths beyond tracing out!" (Romans 11:33). He wants me, instead, to sit at his feet like a weaned child at rest with her mother, humble, content, depending on him to do his great works in Nate (Psalm 131:1–2). As I wait, Jesus gives me a prayer to pray: "Your kingdom come, your will be done, on earth as it is in heaven" (Matthew 6:10).

Thank you, Father, for not letting me stay in Fantasy Land. You gave me a child who shattered my unworthy dreams so that you, who can never disappoint, could fulfill your very great and precious promises in the two of us, both Nate and me.

27

How Much More!

I was praying for Nate recently and thought of Matthew 7:9–11 (from the Sermon on the Mount): "Would any of you offer his son a stone when he asks for bread, or a snake when he asks for a fish? If you, bad as you are, know how to give good things to your children, how much more will your heavenly Father give good things to those who ask him!" (REB).

A similar account is found in Luke 11:11–13. A disciple had asked, "Teach us to pray" (Luke 11:1), and Jesus answered much the same.

What caught my eye in both passages was what Jesus says about you and me. "You, being evil," or "bad as you are," makes it clear that we are unlike God. We can give fairly good gifts to our kids, even to those who are rebelling. But then he contrasts "how much more will the heavenly Father give" (REB). I'm always thinking about how much I love my son and how much I have prayed for him over many years. But how much more does Nate's heavenly Father care about him.

We've provided Nate a roof over his head, clothes, food, love, and every advantage. For his birthday, I sent a Walmart gift card. What if it had been a car? What is that compared to God's perfect gifts, the "how much more" gifts, like peace, joy, freedom from drugs, a home, a job, unfailing love? I think of God's protection of Nate over many years in precarious situations in prison, and currently in his lean-to in the woods. He has also been physically healthy overall and has had regular work with folks who care about him.

Thank you, Father. Help me never to forget how much more you give and long to give to your children.

28

Darn . . . It's So Hard!

These were the exact words I used when our grandson was causing his parents and us such sadness by his stubborn, rebellious ways. He wants to be out on his own. But as a teen, he has little idea of what will come to rest, every day, on his shoulders alone. He is at this awful in-between age. I grieve more, though, for his parents. They are trying to reason with an unreasonable, headstrong young adult. This family upheaval brought back memories of dealing with Nate. Although I had found God faithful to our son, I was still tempted to believe the lie that my grandson's case is hopeless. It is just plain hard to keep trusting.

These fearful thoughts filled my mind as I met a friend in the grocery parking lot that afternoon. In response to her "How are you?" greeting, I shared briefly about my teen trouble. She smiled knowingly and shared with me how she too had been brainless and foolish at that age. That was, until the Lord "hit her with a two-by-four." That blow woke her up and changed her life. What a timely testimony from a former rebel. It was not, however, a promise from God that some stroke would quickly turn *my* grandson around that gave me hope that day. Instead, it was seeing how God responded to my distress and brought comfort right there as I shopped.

29

Pesky What-ifs

Recently I was bombarded with discouraging thoughts:

If I had just known he needed . . .
Had I tried this program . . .
Wow! If I had only known about this guy . . .
That worked for their boy . . .

The list goes on. These are the things that might have been. But wait! God brought to mind the promises in Psalm 139, and as I thought on those truths, he convinced me that every one of the what-ifs touching Nate's life were held tightly in God's hand before time began.

"You saw me before I was born and scheduled each day of my life before I began to breathe. Every day was recorded in your book!

How precious it is, Lord, to realize you are thinking about me constantly. I can't even count how many times a day your thoughts turn toward me. And when I awaken each morning, you are still thinking of me" (Psalm 139:16–18 TLB).

Remembering God's tenderness and meditating on these verses one morning, I put Nate's name in the psalm:

You saw Nate before he was born and scheduled each day of his life before his first breath. Every day of Nate's life was recorded in your book before one of them happened.

How precious it is, Lord, to realize you are thinking about him constantly. I can't even count how many times a day your thoughts turn toward him. And when Nate wakes up each morning, you are still with him (there in that tent in the woods) and thinking such sweet thoughts of him.

Moms, I urge you to believe in God's overwhelming love for your wanderers. You may be in such distress and have been so deeply hurt that you wonder whether you have anything but disgust, anger, and maybe even hatred left for this lost, ugly-acting son or daughter. Psalm 139 reminds us that God loves your child and tells of this love in detail. Put the name of your child, young or old, in the psalm, and read it aloud to the Lord. May he give you new hope for your child as you ponder his great love and care for them.

30

World's End

"Don't fear" doesn't mean we don't get alarmed, that we don't begin thinking hard about the many possibilities that confront us when real trouble comes. But after considering the threats to our lives, we learn to turn our thoughts to the truth that God is mighty in power and love.

When the Twin Towers came down in 2001, Fig and I were in Port Moresby, the capital of Papua New Guinea, waiting for a flight to get medical help in Australia, the nearest country where help is available. It was early morning in PNG when Fig came to our guesthouse room urging me to come see the news. As I walked into the lounge, I saw what seemed like a movie. But it was fact. It showed what had happened eight hours earlier, a plane plowing first into the South Tower, then the North. Terror struck my heart. I was out of my home country, witnessing an attack on that land. In horror my first thought was, *This must be the end of the world!* The second thought is as fresh now as it was in 2001; *Oh, that's right, God is here, God is here, and he's in control!* I was terrified to the point that I had, for a split second, forgotten that the God of heaven is always here, no matter what the horrible facts are.

When you're dealing with a teen acting mindlessly, heedless of danger, it has a horror of its own. We need to know that God is here, not on his way, but here with us and also simultaneously there with our son or daughter. The devil would have us paralyzed by the possibilities of our wanderer's choices. "So, do not fear, for I am with you; do not be dismayed, for I am your God. I will strengthen you and help you; I will uphold you with my righteous right hand" (Isaiah 41:10). We don't have to give in to fear, however frightening our situation. God promises to give us the power to withstand any adversity and resist the Enemy's attacks.

31

Three Right Responses to Your Prodigal

Prayer

What a gift we have in a living Lord who refers to himself as a "hearer of prayer" (Psalm 65:2 REB). He tells us to bring our concerns to him. Then he urges, "Do not be anxious about anything, but in every situation, by prayer and petition, with thanksgiving, present your requests to God" (Philippians 4:6). Why does he tell us this? He knows that when we face tough situations, we panic. We consider the alarming possibilities, and our tummies churn and necks tighten as we scheme how we can right the ship and fix things. God wants us to give these troubles to him and, in peace, turn and look at Jesus. "Let us fix our eyes on Jesus, the pioneer and perfecter of faith. For the joy set before him he endured the cross, scorning its shame, and sat down at the right hand of the throne of God" (Hebrews 12:2). We can leave our wanderer in their Maker's hands. The Great Repairman knows what is broken and has just the plan to make him or her whole. That settled, we focus more of our time and attention on God, instead of worrying about this child. He's promised to answer, so we pray, give thanks, and take a seat at our Father's feet.

Share

As parents, it is important to be part of a group of believers in the God of the Bible. A defiant teen or out-of-control child of any age is unpredictable. So the family tends to withdraw instead of reaching out. We stop having people over and stop going out as a family. It's not worth the hassle. This isolation only makes matters worse as we wallow alone in our perceived failure to repair the struggler. I urge you to be brave and share your heartaches with someone. A good place is a women's Bible Study. We are so sure we're the only one who has such a child, and we feel ashamed. Please know you are not alone. Over the years I've made it a point to share parts of my story in various settings. What I've found is that usually others will then open up about their kids, and together we find comfort (2 Corinthians 1:3–6).

Dare

Dare to trust God. When the pain we feel for our child is paralyzing, and we're on the edge of giving up, consider how much God loves you and your wayward one. He is aware of your desperation and is always near. Admit to him that your dreams for this precious one are small-minded compared to his complex and perfect plans. Look up to that all-knowing, all-loving God, and have courage to give that treasure to him, like Abraham did with Isaac, with an open hand, no strings attached. Although we cannot know God's purposes, we can know God. He is perfectly good. That cannot change (Psalm 119:68). He will treat our children with perfect love and mercy. Dare to trust him, and trust him again.

32

Our Story Continues

This book is at its end, but Nate's story is not. Several years ago I would have wanted to write a book about answered prayer. But in the process of putting together my son's story, my attention was captured by God, whom I found bigger and better in himself than any answers he could have given me. His numerous acts of kindness to Nate convinced me that all of these came out of a plan conceived long before he was born. That same God will remain true, and finish the work he began.

Does this mean that I'm not interested in the particulars of his plan? No. I'm his mom! But I'm a mom who's been persuaded to believe God.

This is my story, this is my song,
Praising my Savior, all the day long.

Acknowledgments

Warm thanks to

The many folks who have prayed for Nate; Pastor Bob, for being there with us at his trial; Larry and Claudia, for hosting us after he was released from prison; Judy and Lorna, for giving Nate years of yard work to keep him busy earning money, and being loved.

Special thanks to

The Book Covers, my prayer team of seven, who were indispensable in this project: Carol, Claudia, Linda, Meg, Miriam, Sammee, and Sara. Besides responding to requests, you were available to listen.

My dear family, who think the world of Nate, and treat him so.

About the Author

Susan Hamlin, Texas born, is a native of Morehead City, North Carolina. She, with her husband Newton, and children Miriam and Nate, spent seventeen years in Papua New Guinea in linguistics and Bible translation. Her self-discipline and warm faithfulness expressed themselves in ready hospitality, decades of praying, and preparing her family fifty-five thousand meals. Her upbringing, her trust in Jesus, and trouble itself, have been effective to give her a heart and a voice.

www.ingramcontent.com/pod-product-compliance
Lightning Source LLC
Chambersburg PA
CBHW020359130626
46549CB00006B/2350